AQA AS Level Philosophy

REVISION GUIDE

Paper 1

K Lancaster

Homunculus Publishing
Unit 44a, Harley Street, Marylebone,
London, W1G 9QE

ISBN: 978-1-912338-94-8

1 2 3 4 5 6 7 8 9 10

CONTENTS

Introduction	**5**
The basics	**7**
Premises and arguments	8
Deductive arguments	11
Inductive arguments	12
Abductive arguments	12
Criticising arguments	13
Fallacies	14
The exam	19
Epistemology	**27**
What is knowledge?	**28**
Tripartite definition of knowledge	29
Necessity	30
Sufficiency: Gettier problems	32
Infallibilism	35
No false lemmas	36
Reliabilism	37
Virtue epistemology	39
Truth-tracking	41
Theories of perception	**42**
Direct realism	43
Indirect realism	47
Idealism	49
Types of possibility and truth	**51**
Sources of knowledge	**56**
Empiricism	57
Innatism	60
Rationalism: intuition and deduction	64
Arguments for the existence of God	68
Proof of the external world	70
Limits of knowledge: scepticism	71

Moral Philosophy	**75**
Moral philosophy basics	**76**
Normative ethics	**78**
Act utilitarianism	78
Rule utilitarianism	81
Preference utilitarianism	83
Other forms of utilitarianism	85
Kantian ethics	86
Virtue ethics	91
Similarities and differences	94
Applied ethics	**95**
Eating animals	95
Simulated killing	98
Lying	101
Stealing	103
Meta ethics	**106**
Moral naturalism	108
Moral non-naturalism	111
Error theory	113
Emotivism	116
Prescriptivism	120
Supplementary material	**123**
Specification content	123
Possible exam questions	129
List of philosophers	133
Set texts and further reading	134
Glossary	136
Index	154

Introduction

How to use this book

This revision textbook covers the entire AS specification. You can read it all the way through, but a better approach is to dip in and out of sections as you revise them, or as you learn them throughout the year.

It is a good idea for you to read 'The Basics' (p7-26) as early as possible, as the information contained within it is vital to your understanding of philosophical arguments, and the exam.

When a term is written in SMALL CAPITALS, you will find it in the glossary on pages 136-153.

Anthology and text translations

AQA provides a list of set philosophical texts (see p134) to allow students to engage directly with philosophers' ideas. Sometimes these texts are written in a style which students find difficult to understand and analyse, but you should not let the language of the set texts put you off studying Philosophy. This book aims to present the ideas in the specification and the set texts to you in a simple yet complete way.

What You Need to Know

The Specification is your guide to what you need to know (see p123-128); you can be asked a question about anything on the Specification. It is worth noting that the Specification does not always give lots of details about a particular area of the syllabus – for example, the applied ethics issues and the moral anti-realist theories are only mentioned as brief bullet points, but it is entirely possible that any of these could arise as an essay question.

Criticisms

Some criticisms are described on the Specification; these are criticisms that you must know as a minimum, as these can specifically be asked about in an exam question. It is useful to know at least four criticisms (or strengths) for each theory, so that you can utilise these in the exam. Knowing four or more criticisms per theory means that you will be able to choose which two or three criticisms are most relevant to the question being asked.

Philosophers' names

There are some philosophers whose names are given on the Specification, and you will need to learn these philosophers' arguments because an exam question could mention them by name. For example:

- Explain René Descartes' notion of 'clear and distinct ideas'. *(5 marks)*

Many of the great philosophers wrote about a wide variety of subjects: you do not need to know all of their arguments – only the ones which are mentioned in the Specification. If know other philosophers or arguments which are relevant to a question, you can still receive credit for knowing these.

If you wish to know when a philosopher was writing, or what their first name was, you can refer to the list on page 133. This list is provided for reference, to help put arguments into historical context. But you do *not need* to remember the life spans, publication years, or first names of any philosopher, *and you will not receive any extra marks for knowing them.*

The Basics Overview

Premises and arguments

- Inferences and arguments:
  - How arguments can be presented
  - Types of premise
  - Antecedents and consequents
- Deductive arguments – conclusions which are entailed by premises
- Inductive arguments – conclusions which are probable
- Abductive arguments – conclusions which are inferences to the best explanation
- Criticising arguments – criticising the premises and the logic
- Fallacies – flawed ways of reasoning which you should avoid

The exam

- Question weighting and assessment objectives
- How the Philosophy exam differs from other exams
- Laying out arguments:
  - Precision
  - Redundancy
- Writing good essays
  - Introductions
  - Conclusions
  - Paragraphs

Premises and Arguments

Overview

This book attempts to provide you with precise arguments so that you can break them down and use them in the exam. Where possible, this is done through arguments set out as PREMISES and CONCLUSIONS. It is important for you to know what is meant by these terms.

- **Premises**: the statements laid out to form part of the argument
- **Conclusion**: a statement which can be derived from the premises
- **Argument**: one or more premises, leading to a conclusion

Inferences and arguments

Drawing a conclusion from one or more premises is called INFERENCE. INDUCTIVE inferences form an inductive argument, while DEDUCTIVE inferences form a deductive argument, and ABDUCTIVE inferences form an INFERENCE TO THE BEST EXPLANATION.

- **Deductive argument**: if the premises are true, the conclusion *must* also be true. This is a way of finding a conclusion which is certain, based on logical reasoning.
- **Inductive argument**: if the premises are true, the conclusion is *likely* to be true. This is a way of finding a probable conclusion, by looking at evidence or experience.
- **Abductive argument**: if the premises are true, the conclusion is the best explanation of them (an inference to the best explanation).

Presenting arguments

An argument consists of one or more claims (PREMISES) and a conclusion. Arguments can be presented as a numbered list of premises, and C for the conclusion; this is called STANDARD FORM, and is the convention used in this book. For example:

1. All border terriers are dogs
2. All dogs are animals

C. Therefore, all border terriers are animals

Where there are INTERMEDIATE CONCLUSIONS (an inference drawn from premises, which is not the end of the argument), these are numbered as premises but begin with the word ‘therefore’ to show you that it is an intermediate conclusion. For example, in the following argument, premise 3 is an intermediate conclusion:

1. All Yorkshire terriers are dogs
2. No dogs are birds
3. Therefore no Yorkshire terriers are birds
4. All swans are birds

C. Therefore, no Yorkshire terriers are swans

An alternative convention (which is not used in this book, but is fine for you to use in exams) is to write arguments as a bulleted list. If you do this, be sure to use 'therefore' to indicate the conclusion.

- All Jack Russell terriers are dogs
- All dogs are mammals
- Therefore, all Jack Russell terriers are mammals

Types of premise

There are different types of premise; a premise may be:

- A statement of fact (e.g. the Holocaust occurred during WW2)
- A generalised statement / assumption (e.g. all people have happy thoughts at some point)
- A definition (e.g. vixens are female foxes)
- A hypothetical statement (e.g. if a person loves God, then he will act morally)

Premises may be explicit or implicit. The EXPLICIT premises are the ones the author actually writes. The IMPLICIT premises are the ones which are clearly being relied upon, but have not been stated outright. In this book, implicit premises have (implied) written before them.

The justification for a premise is usually drawn from evidence or experience (A POSTERIORI). It is also possible to find the truth of some premises without experience (A PRIORI), that is to say, just by thinking about them. These include mathematical truths such as 5 + 2 = 7, and ANALYTIC truths which are usually definitions such as "all bachelors are unmarried men". See pages 51-68 for more information on this.

Subjects and predicates

In a simple statement, there is usually a subject and a predicate. The SUBJECT is the person, animal or object that the statement is about. The PREDICATE is the information about the subject. E.g. in the statement "the fish is big", 'the fish' is the subject, and 'is big' is the predicate. There may be more than one predicate, e.g. "the fish is big, grey and slippery".

Antecedents and consequents

A CONDITIONAL statement is an if-then statement, such as:

- If it's sunny, then I'll wear sunscreen.

The 'if' part of the statement ("it's sunny") is called the ANTECEDENT. The 'then' part of the statement ("I'll wear sunscreen") is called the CONSEQUENT.

Modus ponens

MODUS PONENS is a VALID argument which is sometimes referred to as 'affirming the antecedent'. This means that the writer is saying the 'if' part of the statement is true (typically, the conditional if-then statement is the first premise, and the affirmation – saying the 'if' part is true – is the second premise).

Modus ponens states that: 'If P then Q. P. Therefore Q.' (P and Q are variables which can be substituted for statements). Here is an example:

1. If Sam was born in Canada, then he is Canadian
2. Sam was born in Canada

C. Therefore, Sam is Canadian

Modus tollens

MODUS TOLLENS is a valid argument sometimes referred to as 'denying the consequent'. This means that the writer is saying that the 'then' part of the statement isn't true.

Modus tollens states that: 'If P then Q. Not Q. Therefore not P.' (As noted above, P and Q are variables which can be substituted for statements). Here is an example:

1. If Tom is a doctor, then he must have a medical degree
2. Tom does not have a medical degree

C. Therefore, Tom is not a doctor

Although modus ponens and modus tollens are both deductively VALID forms of argument (if the premises are true, the conclusion must also be true), they bear a resemblance to the FALLACIES of 'affirming the consequent' and 'denying the antecedent' (see p16-17) which means that they can be difficult to spot for students who are new to philosophy.

Deductive Arguments

Overview

Deductive arguments may be invalid, valid or sound.

Invalid arguments

An INVALID ARGUMENT is one where the premises don't ENTAIL the conclusion (there's a problem with the logic – even if the premises were all true, the conclusion could be false.)

Here are two examples of an invalid argument (the premises are true, but the premises don't lead to the conclusion, even though one of the conclusions is true):

1. Vixens are female foxes 2. All fish live in water C. Therefore, foxes are vertebrates	1. Socrates is a man 2. All men are mortal C. Therefore, Socrates is alive today

Valid arguments

A VALID ARGUMENT is one where the premises logically ENTAIL the conclusion (if the premises are true, the conclusion must also be true); it would be a CONTRADICTION for the premises to be true, and the conclusion to be false. A valid argument may have true premises or false premises; if the premises are false or uncertain then the conclusion may also be false or uncertain.

Here are two examples of a valid argument (the premises are false, but they do entail the conclusion; one conclusion is also false):

1. Pork is a vegetable 2. All vegetables are blue C. Therefore, pork is blue	1. All ducks are invertebrates 2. All invertebrates can fly C. Therefore, all ducks can fly

Sound arguments

A SOUND ARGUMENT is one where the premises are all true, and it is valid. A sound argument cannot be refuted (the conclusion is guaranteed to be true).

Here are two examples of a sound argument:

1. Pork comes from dead pigs 2. Pigs are animals C. Therefore, pork comes from dead animals	1. Foxes are mammals 2. No mammals are birds C. Therefore, no foxes are birds

Inductive Arguments

Overview

In an INDUCTIVE ARGUMENT, the premises support the conclusion, but they do not logically ENTAIL it, so it is possible for the premises to be true, and the conclusion to be false. In a good inductive argument, the premises should make the conclusion fairly likely – ideally almost certain (though it can never be 100% certain).

Here is an example of a weak inductive argument:

1. I have seen two octopuses, and they were both grey

C. Therefore, all octopuses are grey

The above argument is weak because it is only based on two observations, yet it generalises to all octopuses.

Here is an example of a stronger inductive argument:

1. I have seen hundreds of swans, and they have all been white

C. Therefore, all swans are white

The above argument seems reasonably strong as it is based on hundreds of observations; however, there are some species of swans which are black, so the conclusion is untrue.

Here is an example of a really strong inductive argument:

1. No human has ever lived beyond the age of 140

C. Therefore, no human will ever live beyond the age of 140

The above argument seems very strong indeed, as it is based on billions of observations (indeed, *all* possible observations), but still the conclusion may not be true, as people may be able to live beyond 140 in the future.

Abductive Arguments

Overview

Abductive arguments are INFERENCES TO THE BEST EXPLANATION. This means that given the facts (which will typically be presented as premises), the conclusion is the best explanation for them. There may be other competing explanations, but the writer asserts that the conclusion is a better explanation than all the other possibilities.

Here is an example of an abductive argument:

1. I know I have a mind
2. I behave in particular ways – when a heavy object hits me, I shout; when a relative dies, I cry; and I can quickly construct new sentences which make grammatical sense
3. Other people display these same behaviours

C. Therefore, other people have minds

In the above argument, the conclusion is not logically entailed by the premises, but the premises do seem to make the conclusion fairly likely (but not certain). There are other competing conclusions, such as that everybody else is mindlessly mimicking my behaviour – but other people having minds seems more plausible.

Criticising Arguments

Overview

Usefulness of arguments

One of the benefits of a valid deductive argument is that the premises guarantee the conclusion, giving us absolute certainty that if the premises are true, the conclusion must also be true. However, their downfall is that they rarely tell us anything new; they merely restate the premises in a shorter, more concise way, as if it is new knowledge, when really that information was contained in the premises all along.

On the other hand, inductive arguments can tell us useful new things about the world, by making generalisations or predictions about future events. However, their downfall is that they can never yield total certainty like deductive arguments can.

Neither deductive nor inductive arguments can prove the truth of their premises, so it is always important for philosophers and students to fact-check the truth of the premises before accepting that the conclusion is true.

Criticising arguments

There are two ways to criticise an argument:

• **Criticise its premises** (e.g. by arguing that one or more premise is false or questionable)	• **Criticise its logic** (e.g. by showing that the premises do not entail the conclusion)

You can of course criticise the premises *and* the logic of an argument. When you approach arguments you come across in Philosophy, it is useful for you to consider these two aspects of an argument separately:

- Consider whether each premise is (absolutely) true – if one or more premises are false, vague or questionable, then the conclusion drawn from them is equally problematic.
- Consider the logic of the argument:
  - If it is a DEDUCTIVE ARGUMENT, is it VALID? Is the conclusion entailed by the premises?
  - If it is an INDUCTIVE ARGUMENT, how likely is the conclusion? Can there be other possible conclusions from the same premises?
  - If it is an ABDUCTIVE ARGUMENT, is the conclusion really the best explanation for the facts? Are there other more likely conclusions?

Be very clear about what you are criticising. Write things like: "Premise 1 can be criticised because…" or "This argument is not deductively valid because…" This helps the examiner to see exactly which aspect of an argument you are challenging, and it will gain higher marks than one which is less clear about what is being criticised.

Fallacies

Overview

A fallacy is a type of faulty reasoning, and even the great philosophers fall victim to them sometimes. Some of the following are not logical fallacies, but all are flawed ways of arguing.

• Circular justification	• Denying the antecedent
• Begging the question	• Fallacy of composition
• Contradictions	• Attacking a straw man

• False dilemma • Affirming the consequent	• Ad hominem • Slippery slope argument

Circular justification

This is where the conclusion relies on the premises, and the premises rely on the conclusion. This forms a circular argument.

Here is an example:

1. Dad says that Mum always tells the truth
2. Therefore Mum does not lie
3. Mum says that Dad always tells the truth

C. Therefore Dad does not lie

Begging the question

This can seem quite similar to circularity. It is when an argument is based on an assumption (often in the conclusion) which an opponent would deny, and the argument uses this assumption within one of its premises.

Here is an example:

1. We are able to study the mind using a brain scanner

C. Therefore, the mind is the same thing as the brain

This is an example of begging the question, because an opponent who believes that the mind is *not* the brain would simply deny that we can study the mind using a brain scanner. The premise is based on the assumption that the conclusion is true.

You should never use the phrase 'beg the question' to mean 'invite discussion of', for example: "Saying that we shouldn't eat animals begs the question of whether we should drink milk." Although people say this type of thing which in conversations, it is technically an incorrect use of 'beg the question' and has no place in a Philosophy essay.

Contradictions

Contradictions can be relatively easy to spot in some short arguments, but in longer and more complex arguments, they are tricky to pick out.

Here is an example:

1. Everything has a cause
2. The universe has a cause
3. The cause of the universe must be uncaused
4. God is the only uncaused entity in existence

C. Therefore, God is the cause of the universe

The contradiction here is between premises 1, 3 and 4 (and the conclusion). If everything has a cause, then God too must have a cause, but the argument proceeds as though this contradiction is acceptable.

False dilemma

A dilemma is presented in the form: 'Either P or Q. Not P. Therefore, Q.' This is can be a VALID FORM of argument such as: "Either Rachael is at home, or she's somewhere else. Rachael isn't at home. Therefore, she's somewhere else."

However, the argument becomes fallacious when the two options presented aren't *really* the only options:

1. Either you support unlimited immigration, or you're a racist bigot
2. You don't support unlimited immigration

C. Therefore, you're a racist bigot

This is a false dilemma, as there is a middle ground between accepting unlimited immigration and being a racist bigot; they aren't the only two possibilities.

Affirming the consequent

This is a fallacy which can be tricky to spot, as it takes a similar form to a valid type of argument known as MODUS PONENS (see p10).

The 'affirming the consequent' fallacy states that: 'If P then Q. Q. Therefore P.' Here is an example:

1. If you have hit the TV with a hammer, then the TV would be broken
2. The TV is broken

C. Therefore, you have hit the TV with a hammer

This is a fallacy because the premises can be true, without guaranteeing the conclusion. There are other possible explanations for 'Q' (the TV being broken) – premise 1 lays out *one possible way* in which the TV could have broken, but it does not state that this is the *only* possible way, which is what is assumed by the conclusion.

Another way of saying this is that premise 1 lays out a SUFFICIENT CONDITION for the TV being broken, but it is not a NECESSARY CONDITION.

Denying the antecedent

This is another fallacy which can be tricky to spot, as it takes a similar form to a valid type of argument known as MODUS TOLLENS (see p10).

The 'denying the antecedent' fallacy states that: 'If P then Q. Not P. Therefore not Q.' Here is an example:

1. If you have been in a car crash, then you have been in a car
2. You have not been in a car crash

C. Therefore, you have not been in a car

This is a fallacy because the premises can be true, without guaranteeing the conclusion. Just because 'P' isn't the case (you haven't been in a car crash) doesn't prove that 'Q' isn't the case (you haven't been in a car). Another way of saying this is that premise 1 lays out a NECESSARY CONDITION for being in a car crash, but it is not a SUFFICIENT CONDITION (you can be in a car without being in a car crash).

Fallacy of composition

The fallacy of composition is an incorrect assumption that because something is true of particular examples, the same thing must be true of the group as a whole.

This is easier to demonstrate with a couple of examples:

1. All the parts of the human body have a particular function

C. Therefore, the human body as a whole has a function

1. There is a reason why ladybirds are red
2. There is a reason why blood is red

C. Therefore, there is a (single) reason why *both of them* are red

Just because various things share a feature – e.g. the feature of redness or of having a function – does not mean that the group of things as a whole has that particular feature.

Attacking a straw man

This is not a logical fallacy, but it is a poor way of arguing. It involves distorting or misrepresenting an argument (usually one you disagree with), and then criticising that distorted argument. For example:

Kant argues that:

1. When you do an action, everyone else will do that action too
2. If everyone doing that action will cause chaos, then it's wrong to do it
3. If everyone tried to catch the 1 o'clock train, it would cause chaos

C. Therefore, it's morally wrong to get the 1 o'clock train

This is a poor argument from Kant, because ...

This is an example of attacking a straw man, because Kant's argument has been distorted or misinterpreted (whether intentionally or unintentionally), and then the distorted version is being criticised.

When you present a philosopher's argument, it is important to adhere to their actual argument, rather than a watered-down or confused version. If you distort their argument into something with questionable premises and/or poor logic, then you are not doing them justice – and you will lose marks for it. To avoid attacking a straw man, learn philosophers' arguments as accurately as possible.

Ad hominem

This is not a fallacy, but simply a poor way of arguing. An 'ad hominem' criticism means that you are attacking the person, rather than their argument. In Philosophy, we should stick to criticising arguments, rather than the people themselves. Here is an example of an ad hominem criticism:

Socrates argued that mathematics was innate, but we shouldn't believe this, because Socrates was put to death for corrupting the youth, and we shouldn't accept the words of a criminal.

Slippery slope argument

This is not a fallacy, but it can be a poor way of arguing. A slippery slope argument suggests that if we allow a small act, then we're stepping onto a 'slippery slope' which will lead onto bigger, more troublesome acts.

If we help paralysed, terminally ill people to take their own lives, this will lead on to other types of euthanasia, and we will end up with people murdering disabled people against their will and calling it euthanasia.

If we legalise cannabis, then people will start using it more, and this will lead them onto harder drugs, until they become heroin addicts.

The slippery slope argument is problematic because it isn't always true that allowing a small-scale act will always lead onto the bigger, more troublesome acts.

The Exam

Overview

In the AS Philosophy exam (Paper 1 of the A Level), you will answer 10 questions, consisting of 5 on Epistemology, and 5 on Moral Philosophy.

Epistemology	Moral Philosophy
1. What is... (2 marks)	6. What is... (2 marks)
2. Explain... (5 marks)	7. Explain... (5 marks)
3. Outline and explain... (9 marks)	8. Outline and explain... (9 marks)
4. Outline and explain... (9 marks)	9. Outline and explain... (9 marks)
5. Critically assess... (15 marks)	10. Critically assess... (15 marks)

Timing

- *Duration of exam*: 3 hours (180 minutes)
- *Total marks available*: 80

This equates to around 2-3 minutes per mark, though you will probably work more quickly than this on the shorter questions, and allow more time for the longer questions.

There is no perfect amount to write for each question; it's the *content* of the writing which gains the marks, rather than the amount itself. So use the table below as a *rough* guide, not a hard-and-fast rule.

Total marks	AO1	AO2	Time to spend	Amount to write
2 marks	2	0	3 minutes	1-2 sentences
5 marks	5	0	10 minutes	3-6 sentences
9 marks	9	0	20 minutes	½-1 side of A4
9 marks	9	0	20 minutes	½-1 side of A4
15 marks	7	8	35 minutes	2 sides of A4

Assessment objectives

Assessment objectives (AOs) are the different skills you are being assessed on in the exam.

- *AO1: Knowledge and understanding.* You must demonstrate knowledge and understanding of the core concepts and methods of philosophy, including the use of philosophical analysis.
- *AO2: Analysis and evaluation.* You must analyse and evaluate philosophical arguments to form reasoned judgements.

In questions worth 2, 5, and 9 marks, all the marks are AO1 marks. This means that you are assessed on your knowledge and understanding of philosophers' arguments, concepts, theories and so on. In these questions, you need to demonstrate that you can clearly and precisely articulate the arguments in question; you are not required to input your own opinion or argument into these shorter questions. (If the question asks you for a criticism, then you have some autonomy to choose which criticism you will explain, but there is little independence beyond this.)

In the 15-mark essays, there are 7 AO1 marks, and 8 AO2 marks. This means that you are assessed on your knowledge and understanding (see above) as well as your ability to analyse and evaluate philosophers' arguments. You will need to put forward strengths and criticisms of theories, weigh them up, and reach a reasoned conclusion. This requires more independence of thought, and you are required to input your own opinion into the essay. See pages 129-132 for some possible questions.

Philosophy and other subjects

Many social science and humanities subjects require students to write essays and to answer short questions as a form of assessment. However, the requirements of many other subjects are different from the requirements of Philosophy:

Many other subjects	Philosophy
1. Often expect you to write for almost the entire duration of the exam.	1. Does not expect you to write for the entire duration of the exam. You might spend up to a third of your time planning, thinking and editing.
2. Often expect you to produce perhaps 6-8 sides of writing for a 1.5 hour exam.	2. Does not expect you to produce 6-8 sides of writing; 3-4 sides (in 1.5 hours) may be sufficient to achieve highly if your answers are well-crafted.
3. Do not usually expect perfection and may overlook small errors.	3. Precision is valued over the amount you write; a shorter but more accurate answer can score highly. Beware of making silly errors which will lose you marks.
4. If a question asks for two reasons and you give three (correct) reasons, you do not lose marks.	4. If a question asks for two reasons and you give three (correct) reasons, you can lose marks.

5. Require you to write in "continuous prose" i.e. full sentences and paragraphs throughout (especially in essays). (Ensure you check these guidelines with your other subjects.)	5. Essays should consist primarily of continuous prose, but bulleted or numbered lists, flowcharts or diagrams are permitted (and even encouraged) within essays, or as an entire response to a shorter question. This is particularly true if a list or diagram is the most precise way to present an argument (see below).

Laying out answers

Consider these different ways in which you could answer the following question:

- Explain the argument from illusion. *(5 marks)*

Response 1:

The argument from illusion states that our senses can deceive us, such as a straight rod in water appearing to be bent. But direct realists suggest that our senses are always accurately telling us about the world. So given that our senses can deceive us about the rod in water, this shows that direct realism isn't true.

Response 2:

1. A straight rod immersed in water appears to be bent
2. If something appears bent when really it is straight, we are not perceiving it accurately
3. Direct realism argues that we perceive the world accurately

C. Therefore, direct realism is false

Response 3:

A straight rod in water appears bent	→	If something which is straight appears to be bent, we are not perceiving it accurately	→	Direct realism argues that we perceive the world accurately	→	Direct realism is false

The three responses above are all saying similar things, but the second and third responses are more precise.

Precision

Precision is very important in the Philosophy exam, and the mark schemes make frequent references to it; it is particularly important in the shorter (2, 5, and 9 mark) questions.

Examiners use the word "precision" to mean being accurate (getting the wording exactly correct) and being concise (keeping to the point and not waffling). The aim is that your answers are correct, clear, succinct, you 'hit the nail on the head', and you avoid vagueness and 'waffle'.

Consider Response 4 to the same question as above; it is *not* precise, and would lose some marks compared to responses 2 and 3 above.

Response 4:

The argument from illusion is part of direct realism which is a theory of perception about the way we see the world. It thinks that our eyes can play tricks on us sometimes and cause an optical illusion. For example, if we put a rod in water then it might seem to bend. This shows that the water has tricked our eyes and made things look different. Direct realists can't explain why this occurs.

There are numerous problems with Response 4, where the writer has been vague and hasn't clearly answered the question. For example, it is misleading to identify the argument from illusion as 'part of' direct realism, when it is actually a criticism of direct realism. If someone who had never studied Philosophy were to read Response 4, they would still not really understand what the argument from illusion was, because Response 4 is confused rather than precise. The references to optical illusions and the water 'tricking our eyes' are not accurate.

Redundancy

If you have accurately answered the question, then simply adding more information isn't automatically going to improve your answer – in fact, it may detract from it, as the extra material may be redundant.

The mark schemes use the word "redundancy" to refer to irrelevant or unnecessary information in an exam response. Redundancy can demonstrate uncertainty, and should therefore be avoided as it can lose you marks. Consider this response to the same question as above:

Response 5:

Our senses can deceive us – e.g. a straight rod in water appears bent. Direct realism argues that we perceive the world accurately and directly, so if something straight appears to be bent, then direct realism is false. A table can appear different when you move about the room – it looks like a dark brown rectangle from one angle, but a light brown diamond from another angle. The table isn't really changing – just our perceptions of it. Also, hallucinations aren't real, but they appear to be real. So direct realism is false.

This is not a good response because all of the material from "A table..." onwards is redundant. The response explains the argument from illusion – but it also (briefly) explains the argument from perceptual variation, and it mentions the argument from hallucination. This gives the impression that the candidate does not really know what the argument from illusion is, and they are simply trying to write lots of things in the hope that one of them is right. The response would score more highly if the material from "A table..." onwards were omitted.

Some GCSE and A-Level mark schemes will award full marks if the correct answer appears in amongst irrelevant material. But it is perfectly reasonable to award a lower mark to a candidate who is uncertain of the answer, and a higher mark to one who gives the right answer but nothing more. If someone asked the question: "What is 3 + 4?" and person A responded by saying: "Six, seven, eight, nine" and person B responded by saying "Seven," then it would seem fair that person B gets more credit for their answer than person A. This is how the Philosophy exam works.

If you are thinking of including extra information which doesn't help to clarify or support your answer, then it is probably be best to omit it: this applies to questions worth 2, 5 and 9 marks in particular.

15 mark essays

With the 15 mark essays there is more room for manoeuvre than with the shorter questions. Of course, if an entire paragraph is irrelevant then it should be omitted; however, being concise is less of an issue, as you will be writing far more. It is important for your arguments to be supported by examples or evidence, rather than being mere assertions.

As noted on p20, you should mostly write in continuous prose, but it is acceptable to lay out an argument in STANDARD FORM within your essay.

What's important

The mark schemes note that the best essays are ones where...

"The student argues with clear and sustained intent. A complete and coherent argument leads to a clear conclusion. The content is detailed and correct and sufficient material is selected and deployed to answer the question fully. The conclusion is arrived at through a balancing of arguments, with appropriate weight given to each argument and to the argument overall. Where there are crucial arguments, these are distinguished from less crucial ones... Philosophical language is used consistently and correctly throughout."

But what does this all mean?

- "Arguing with clear intent" means that you need to clearly argue for one position or another. In most cases, it doesn't matter which side of a debate you argue in favour of – it only matters that you clearly argue for one particular side of the debate. For example, you could argue that all knowledge comes from experience, or that not all knowledge comes from experience. If you are not sure which side to argue in favour of, then simply pick one side and argue for it – never have an argument which is vague or indecisive.
- "Balancing of arguments" does not mean that you need to have an equal number of strengths and criticisms, but merely that you need to consider both sides of the debate to some extent.
- "Distinguishing crucial arguments" means that it is not sufficient to merely explain a criticism – in addition, you must comment on how strong the criticism is. You should highlight whether the criticism is only a small problem for the theory in question, or whether it renders the theory wholly unworkable.
- "Philosophical language" means that where possible, you should use key terms (see p136-153).

Introductions and conclusions

Your 15-mark essays should argue towards a clear conclusion. You should always outline your conclusion in the introduction – this isn't a movie; your essay doesn't need a surprise ending! Ideally, the introduction and conclusion should 'mirror' each other – i.e. they should closely resemble one another, and can even use similar wording.

A poor conclusion is one which doesn't really answer the question, or one which concludes that it's all a matter of opinion and people can believe whatever they want to believe. Below are some examples of introductions and conclusions:

Poor introduction:	Good introduction:
In this essay I will assess empiricism, and I will compare it with innatism and rationalism. I will consider arguments for and against each side, and reach a conclusion.	In this essay I will argue that the empiricist claim that all knowledge comes from experience is flawed and implausible, due to the existence of a priori knowledge which can be obtained through reason alone.

Poor conclusion:	**Good conclusion:**
In this essay I have evaluated empiricism. I have shown that there are arguments for empiricism and arguments against it, such as the existence of innate knowledge, and the idea that we are a blank slate at birth. Rationalism and empiricism both have their strengths and weaknesses – it's down to personal opinion which theory people want to agree with.	In this essay I have examined the empiricist claim that all knowledge comes from experience, and demonstrated that such a claim is flawed and implausible. I acknowledged that although much of our knowledge comes from experience, there is some a priori knowledge which can be obtained through reason alone, and that is sufficient to demonstrate that the empiricists are wrong to claim that <u>all</u> knowledge comes from experience.

It should be clear from the phrasing used in the essay – particularly the introduction and the conclusion – exactly what question is being answered. Hopefully when you read the good introduction and good conclusion above, you can spot that the question being answered is "Critically assess the empiricist claim that all knowledge comes from experience". You can tell this because the words from the question are used in the answer; this helps to demonstrate to the examiner that you are actually answering the question.

The poor introduction and conclusion are vague and noncommittal, and it is not really clear what question is being answered, nor what answer the student is trying to give.

The middle part of essays

Of course, you need more than just a good introduction and conclusion – the middle part of an essay also needs to be good. You need to explain theories, but you should devote most of your time to evaluation. You should prioritise depth of evaluation over breadth: the best approach is to cover no more than three evaluative points, but to cover these in depth – you could cover just two evaluative points if you wish to discuss one or more lengthy replies. Do not try to shoehorn eight simplistic and undeveloped evaluative points into your essay; this will not achieve a good mark.

Where possible, use key terms (see p136-153) as it will help to make your argument more precise. You should link each paragraph to the question (ideally using words from the question) so it is clear how that paragraph helps to answer the question. Remember also to comment on how crucial the criticism is (see previous page).

Poor paragraph	Good paragraph
Some philosophers have demonstrated that there is some knowledge which does not need experience – rather, it can be known automatically. For example, you know you exist simply by thinking about it. Moreover, this is not simply a meaningless truth.	Rationalists have demonstrated that there is some knowledge which is not a posteriori – rather, it can be known a priori through reason alone. For example, the cogito ("I think therefore I am") can be known simply by thinking about it. Moreover, this is not merely a trivial analytic truth, but a synthetic a priori proposition. This criticism deals a devastating blow to the empiricist claim that all knowledge comes from experience, because it is a substantive truth which can be known a priori.

The good paragraph has accurately used terms such as 'rationalists', 'synthetic a priori' and 'substantive truth' which help to demonstrate understanding, and they make the answer more precise. By contrast, the poor paragraph has used vague and confused terms such as 'known automatically' and 'meaningless truth'. The good paragraph has also commented on the strength of the criticism ("This criticism deals a devastating blow…") whereas the poor paragraph has not indicated whether the criticism is a strong one or a weak one; they have just left the reader to work it out for themselves.

It is never a good technique to leave it to the examiner to 'fill in the blanks'; the examiner will of course be able to tell whether your criticism is a strong one or a weak one, but you need demonstrate that *you* know whether it is a strong one or a weak one. If you don't write it, the examiner will assume you don't know it.

Epistemology Overview

What is knowledge?

- Types of knowledge – ability, acquaintance and propositional
- The tripartite definition of knowledge – knowledge is a justified true belief
- Gettier problems – when a JTB isn't knowledge
- Strengthening the definition of knowledge:
  - Infallibilism – beliefs must be infallible to be knowledge
  - No false lemmas – reasoning cannot be based on false premises
  - Reliabilism – agents must use a reliable method of justification
  - Virtue epistemology – the agent must be a person who is skilled in finding knowledge
  - Truth-tracking – beliefs must be sensitive to the truth

Theories of perception

- Direct realism – the external world is exactly as it appears
- Indirect realism – the external world is similar to how it appears, but some qualities which we perceive aren't inherent features of objects
- Idealism – the external world only exists if it is being perceived

Empiricism and rationalism

- Types of possibility and truth
- Sources of knowledge:
  - Empiricism – we acquire knowledge via experience
  - Innatism – we are born knowing some things
  - Rationalism (intuition and deduction) – we acquire knowledge via reasoning

The limits of knowledge

- Arguments for the existence of God
- Proof of the external world – because God would not deceive us
- Limits of knowledge – scepticism

What is Knowledge?

Overview

There are different types of knowledge, and different ways of defining knowledge. When we say "Ellie knows X" what do we mean?

Types of knowledge

There are three types of knowledge:

- ACQUAINTANCE KNOWLEDGE – knowing a person, or knowing attributes about them, as in "I know Jack".
- ABILITY KNOWLEDGE – knowing how to do something such as how to ballet dance or drive a car.
- PROPOSITIONAL KNOWLEDGE – knowing facts or knowing that something is the case, such as knowing that Russia is the world's largest country, or knowing that Nathan is wearing a red hat.

Zagzebski notes that propositional knowledge can be transferred from one person to another, whereas acquaintance knowledge and ability knowledge cannot (or at least, it is much more complicated to transfer ability or acquaintance knowledge from one person to another).

Epistemology is mainly concerned with propositional knowledge: what does it mean for someone to know something, as opposed to believing it? What is the difference between knowledge and a lucky guess?

Defining knowledge

Zagzebski argues that knowledge is achieved when the individual is in 'cognitive contact' with reality. So knowledge is a particular type of relationship between the knower (and his state of mind) and a portion of reality he is acquainted with.

A PROPOSITION such as "I am wearing two shoes" can be true or false – if it is true, then it links the knower with reality in the right sort of way, namely, a true way.

Considerations about truth and reality are METAPHYSICAL questions which we don't generally concern ourselves with in EPISTEMOLOGY. Instead, we focus on the state of mind of the individual (is he certain / confused / aware of his belief?) and the nature of the belief he has (is it true / false / lucky?)

How propositional knowledge can be analysed

In an analysis of knowledge, the use of examples and COUNTER-EXAMPLES is really important. If there is a particular definition of knowledge which has a counter-example to it, then this makes the definition less convincing. A counter-example is one which adheres to the conditions of the definition, but we would not want to class it as knowledge.

For example, if a philosopher defines knowledge as a true belief, but there is an example of someone possessing a true belief, but not knowledge, then this shows that the definition is flawed.

Tripartite Definition of Knowledge

Overview — **Key philosopher:** Plato

Plato defines knowledge as a JUSTIFIED TRUE BELIEF (JTB). It's called the tripartite definition because it has three parts to it:

Justification	Truth	Belief
The belief must be justified (i.e. there must be good reason(s) for having the belief).	The belief must be true. There can be no such thing as 'false knowledge'.	The agent must believe the proposition.

Plato's approach defines knowledge as:

S has knowledge if and only if:

- P is true
- S believes that P
- S is justified in believing that P

The letter S stands for a subject (person) and the letter P is a proposition (statement). Philosophers use the term 'IF AND ONLY IF' (which is commonly abbreviated to 'iff') to indicate NECESSARY AND SUFFICIENT CONDITIONS. Plato asserts that justification, truth and belief are individually necessary and jointly sufficient to be called knowledge. This means that each of the three components of the definition (namely justification, truth, and belief) is needed; when all three appear together, they are adequate to be called knowledge.

It's useful to lay out the necessary and sufficient conditions of knowledge like this, because it allows us to consider all its constituent parts, and ask questions such as these:

1. Is truth necessary? Can someone know something that isn't true?
2. Is justification necessary? Can someone know something without any justification, or with poor justification?
3. Is belief necessary? Can someone know something without believing it, or fully believing it?
4. Are truth, justification and belief jointly sufficient? Is it possible for someone to have a justified true belief (JTB) which is not knowledge?

Note that questions 1-3 are considering whether the conditions are *necessary* for knowledge, whereas question 4 is considering whether the conditions are *sufficient*. Do not mix these up in the exam, as they are separate issues: if a question asks about sufficient conditions, do not discuss which conditions are necessary!

Necessity

Overview

Plato argues that truth, justification and belief are individually necessary for knowledge, but are they? Could someone know something without believing it, without it being true, or without having good justification?

Belief

Some philosophers argue that belief isn't a necessary condition for knowledge, because you can know something without believing it. For example:

Callum takes part in a test, and although he thinks he doesn't know the answers, he actually possesses knowledge that he is unaware of, and he is able to seemingly guess answers with remarkable precision. He had knowledge that he wasn't consciously aware of; he had knowledge without belief.

Some philosophers argue that in order for an agent to know something, they need to *know* that they know it; others argue that an agent can still know something without *knowing* that they know it.

INCOMPATIBILISM argues that belief and knowledge are incompatible – i.e. that if you know something, you don't (merely) believe it; people say things like "I don't just *believe* that you're lying – I *know* you're lying."

Nonetheless, almost all philosophers maintain that belief is a necessary condition for knowledge.

Truth

The truth condition is relatively straightforward, as it is absolutely necessary for knowledge to be true. Centuries ago, people had many incorrect beliefs, such as the belief that the Earth was flat, and that everything is made up of four elements: earth, air, fire and water. Millions of people believed these things, but no one *knew* these things, because they are not true. There can be no such thing as 'false knowledge' – only false beliefs.

If you wish to enter into a discussion, you might mention that we cannot be certain whether we have found 'truth'. For example:

Amy believes in evolution, and there is a lot of evidence for it, so she has a justified belief. But is it true? She can try to find out whether it's true by collecting lots more evidence, but this is just more justification – how can she obtain *truth*?

It seems that only someone from an external perspective – such as God – can say for sure whether people's beliefs are true, and there is no way for us to prove a great deal of our propositional knowledge. There may be a handful of INFALLIBLE beliefs which are incapable of being proven false, but the vast majority of what we think is true, could potentially be proven false.

Despite this minor discussion point, it is unwise to attempt to argue in the exam that someone can have 'false knowledge' or that 'it is true for them' – be absolutely clear that there cannot be false knowledge.

Justification

The issue of whether justification is necessary for knowledge is much more complex than the belief and truth conditions. Some issues include:

- How high should we set the standard for justification – must a belief be INFALLIBLE? (see p35)
- Must the justification be TRUTH-TRACKING? (see p41)
- Is experiencing something adequate justification? (see p57)
- Can an INNATE belief provide adequate justification? (see p60)
- Does logical reasoning provide adequate justification? (see p64)

There is a spectrum of justification: it can range from no justification at all; through very weak evidence; mediocre evidence; good evidence; to exceptionally strong evidence. The difficulty for philosophers is deciding where to draw the line to say that something is adequate justification, whereas something else is not.

So is justification necessary?

Philosophers generally agree that good justification is a necessary condition for knowledge, although they disagree about what good justification actually consists of.

Sufficiency: Gettier Problems

Overview

Key philosopher: Gettier

Gettier puts forward two arguments which challenge the TRIPARTITE DEFINITION OF KNOWLEDGE by demonstrating that justification, truth and belief are not jointly SUFFICIENT for knowledge.

Gettier problems

Gettier outlines two different COUNTER-EXAMPLES to Plato's tripartite definition:

- Job interview (Smith and Jones) example
- Brown in Barcelona example

Examples in the same style as Gettier's (where the belief was true by mere chance, and the justification was unrelated to the truth) are known as 'Gettier problems' or 'Gettier examples'.

Job interview (Smith and Jones)

Gettier's job interview example shows that if someone has a justified belief which is true by luck alone, then this is not knowledge.

- Smith and Jones go to a job interview. Jones looks sure to get the job, and Jones has 10 coins in his pocket
- Smith forms the justified belief 'the man who will get the job has 10 coins in his pocket'
- Then – surprisingly – Smith gets the job!
- It so happens that when Smith looks in his pocket, he too has 10 coins (he didn't know this before)
- So Smith has a JTB that 'the man who will get the job has 10 coins in his pocket'

All three conditions of the tripartite definition have been fulfilled:

- *Belief:* Smith held the belief that 'the man who will get the job has 10 coins in his pocket', so the belief condition was fulfilled.
- *Truth:* The man who got the job (Smith) did indeed have 10 coins in his pocket, so the truth condition was fulfilled.
- *Justification:* Smith had good justification that the man who would get the job had 10 coins in his pocket (because Jones was best friends with the manager, and Smith had seen Jones count out 10 coins) so the justification condition was fulfilled.

So Smith had a JTB, but we would be reluctant to say that he possessed knowledge; therefore a JTB is not sufficient for knowledge.

Brown in Barcelona

Gettier's Brown in Barcelona example also shows that if a JTB is true by mere luck, then this is not knowledge.

- Smith is certain that Jones owns a Ford (Jones has always owned a Ford, and Smith has seen Jones driving in a Ford, and so on)
- Smith does not know Brown's whereabouts, but he forms three beliefs where he picks places at random:
  - (a) Either Jones owns a Ford, or Brown is in Boston
  - (b) Either Jones owns a Ford, or Brown is in Barcelona
  - (c) Either Jones owns a Ford, or Brown is in Brest-Litovsk
- Smith is justified in all three of these beliefs, since he is certain that Jones owns a Ford
- In fact, Jones doesn't own a Ford
- By chance, it turns out that Brown actually *is* in Barcelona, so Smith's belief (b) is true (the other two are false)
- So Smith has a JTB that 'either Jones owns a Ford, or Brown is in Barcelona'

For this example, it should be clear to us that Smith was justified in believing all three propositions – not because of any intuitions he has about where *Brown* is, but because he is certain that Jones owns a Ford. For any DISJUNCTIVE (either-or) statement, we only need to be sure of one half of the statement in order to be sure of the whole statement. (People use this same logic when they say things like "Either you're lying, or pigs can fly" to mean *'You are lying'*. If they are fairly sure you're lying, then the part about pigs flying doesn't need to be true in order for the whole statement to be true.)

All three conditions of the tripartite definition have been fulfilled:

- *Belief:* Smith held the belief that 'either Jones owns a Ford, or Brown is in Barcelona', so the belief condition was fulfilled.
- *Truth:* Brown was indeed in Barcelona, so even though Jones didn't own a Ford, the truth condition was fulfilled.
- *Justification:* Smith had good justification that 'either Jones owns a Ford, or Brown is in Barcelona' (because Jones has always owned a Ford, and he's been seen driving a Ford) so the justification condition was fulfilled.

So Smith had a JTB, but we would be reluctant to say that he possessed knowledge; therefore a JTB is not sufficient for knowledge.

Fake Barns

In both of Gettier's examples, the truth of the proposition is merely due to luck, since the justification for the belief is not caused by the facts, but rather, by some sort of mistake, assumption or guesswork.

Goldman constructs a slightly different type of example – one where a person has a JTB, and the justification *is* related to the facts... but luck is still involved. Here is Goldman's example:

Henry is driving through the countryside in Barn County, and he looks into a field, and sees what looks exactly like a barn. He forms the belief "there is a barn in that field". He is correct that there is a barn in the field, and the thing he is looking at is indeed a barn. However, he is unaware that in Barn County, many farmers construct fake barns – façades which look like real barns when viewed from the road, but are in fact just two-dimensional pictures. Henry got lucky in that he viewed the only real barn for miles around.

The fake barn example is a very tricky one for philosophers to answer, because it appears to be genuine knowledge; Henry saw a real barn, and correctly formed the JTB that it was a real barn – there seems to be no issue here at all. The only problem is that in Barn County he *could* have looked at other barns and thought they were real when they weren't.

Because of the high chance of looking at a fake barn in Barn County, philosophers are usually unwilling to admit that Henry's belief that 'there is a barn in that field' is knowledge – even though it is a JTB with no mistaken reasoning. It was just luck that Henry happened to form the belief when looking at that particular (real) barn, and not one of the fake ones.

Some responses to Gettier-type problems follow below; some are more successful than others. However, few of the theories adequately respond to the problem of fake barns.

Strengthening the definition of knowledge

There are various attempts to solve the issues which Gettier raises (and thus to redefine knowledge):

1. Increase the level of certainty about a belief (INFALLIBILISM) (I + B)
2. Introduce a 'NO FALSE LEMMAS' condition (J + T + B + NFL)
3. Replace 'justified' with 'reliably informed' (RELIABILISM) (R + T + B)
4. Define what makes someone skilled at knowing (VIRTUE EPISTEMOLOGY) (V + T + B)
5. Introduce a 'TRUTH-TRACKING' condition (J + T + B + TT)

Infallibilism

Overview — **Key philosopher:** Descartes

Infallibilism is a response to Gettier's argument that a JTB is not sufficient for knowledge; it focuses on strengthening the 'truth' condition. Merely believing a proposition to be true seems like a fairly weak feeling; being certain of a belief seems like a good way to improve our definition of knowledge.

Philosophers such as Descartes take certainty to a whole different level, requiring beliefs to be so certain that they are INFALLIBLE. If something is infallible, it cannot be wrong. It's not just that the individual *feels* certain about it, but that the proposition *itself* is certain; it is incapable of being wrong. Very few beliefs fit into this category, but some of these are:

- Mathematical truths such as 2 + 2 = 4
- Geometric truths such as 'triangles have three sides'
- Truths about your own existence such as 'I exist'
- ANALYTIC TRUTHS such as 'bachelors are unmarried men'

This approach defines knowledge as:

S has knowledge if and only if: • P is infallible • S believes that P	
In other words, knowledge is an infallible belief; 'infallible' can replace 'true', because if something is infallible then it is definitely true; it cannot be false. We don't need to say it's infallible *and* it's true, because truth is contained within the concept of infallibility. Similarly, we don't need to include 'justification', because the infallibility of a belief is in itself justification for believing it. This can be written as I + B, where I means 'infallible'.	
Strength	**Criticism**
• Infallibilism would be a successful solution to Gettier problems, as it would argue that Smith didn't have knowledge, because there was room for doubt in his beliefs.	• Infallibilism sets the requirements for knowledge so high that almost nothing can be known. Other than mathematical and analytic truths, and knowing that we exist, there are very few SUBSTANTIVE propositions which we can know for sure. Almost all SYNTHETIC TRUTHS are unknowable if we have infallibility as a necessary condition for knowledge.

No False Lemmas

Overview

'No false lemmas' is a response to Gettier's argument that a JTB is not sufficient for knowledge; it adds another condition to the JTB definition. In Gettier's job interview example, we feel reluctant to say that Smith possessed knowledge, because it was pure chance that his belief turned out to be true. Smith's reasoning was like this:

1. Jones has 10 coins
2. Jones is going to get the job

C. Therefore the man who will get the job has 10 coins

A 'lemma' is an assumption or belief which supports a premise, and reasoning which is based on a false LEMMA (a false premise) is not trustworthy. Smith's belief (C) was based on a false lemma (premise 2) that Jones was going to get the job.

So one way of strengthening the definition of knowledge, and solving Gettier problems, is to add a 'no false lemmas' condition to the necessary and sufficient conditions for knowledge.

This approach defines knowledge as:

S has knowledge if and only if:

- P is true
- S believes that P
- S is justified in believing that P
- S's reasoning was not based on any false lemmas

In other words, knowledge is a justified true belief, with no false lemmas. This can be written as J + T + B + NFL, where NFL means no false lemmas.

Strength

- The no false lemmas condition would solve both of Gettier's problems, because both were instances of a JTB based on a false lemma (namely that Jones would get the job, and that Jones owns a Ford).

Criticisms

- The 'no false lemmas' condition does not solve the fake barn problem, as Henry's belief that 'there is a barn in that field' was not based on a false lemma, so his JTB would be counted as knowledge.
- It is not always easy to spot a false lemma when you are the one forming the belief. For example, imagine that you look at a church clock which says 11:45 and you form the JTB that it is 11:45. Unknown to you, the clock had stopped – but by chance, you looked at it when the real time was exactly 11:45. You had a false lemma that 'the clock is telling the right time', but you may never realise it.

Reliabilism

Overview

Reliabilism is a response to Gettier's argument that a JTB is not sufficient for knowledge; it focuses on strengthening the 'justification' condition. PROCESS RELIABILISM is a theory which states that justification is only *good* justification if it is acquired through a reliable process. It cannot be mere accident or luck that S believes that P.

However, reliabilists disagree on what sources or methods of acquiring beliefs are to count as reliable. Some possibilities may include:

1. *Senses* – generally (though not always) our senses give us accurate information about the way the world is. If you can see an elephant in front of you, then this seems to be a reliable process of reaching the belief that 'there is an elephant in front of me'.	2. *Reliable sources* – there are reliable people and reliable sources; if you want to know what elephants eat, then an encyclopedia or an elephant expert are reliable sources, whereas watching the cartoon *'Dumbo'* is not a reliable source.
3. *Memory* – unless something is happening to us right now, we must rely on our memory of what we sensed or what sources we have gained information from. Generally (though not always) our memories seem reasonably reliable.	4. *Inference* – if we have worked from premises to a conclusion, then the conclusion should be true. However, the premises may be based on the senses, memory, or information from reliable sources.

This approach defines knowledge as:

S has knowledge if and only if:

- P is true
- S believes that P
- S's belief that P was arrived at through a reliable process

In other words, knowledge is a true belief which was arrived at through reliable process. This can be written as R + T + B, where R (a reliable process) replaces justification which may not have been obtained through a reliable method.

Strength	**Criticism**
• Requiring a reliable method of reaching beliefs seems sensible in order to exclude cases where people use poor or biased evidence as justification.	• Reliability is highly subjective, and therefore debatable. Emily may think that information on the news is a reliable source, whereas Roshni may think that all news media is constructed to make money and reinforce political ideologies, so the news is unreliable as it's never impartial.

Criticisms

- Process reliabilism doesn't seem to solve Gettier cases particularly well, because Smith did reach his beliefs – both about the job interview and about Jones owning a Ford – through fairly reliable processes (it's just that the belief happened to be true due to some other event).
- Reliabilism doesn't solve fake barn cases, since Henry reached his belief via a (fairly) reliable process – trusting his senses.
- The senses are FALLIBLE (see p44-47) and they can lead us to incorrect beliefs.
- Reliable sources or people are rarely 100% reliable.
- Memory can play tricks on us so that we don't always remember things accurately.
- INDUCTIVE and ABDUCTIVE arguments don't guarantee truth of the conclusion, and even a DEDUCTIVE ARGUMENT is only as good as its premises – if the premises are false, the conclusion is doubtful.

Virtue Epistemology

Overview

VIRTUE EPISTEMOLOGY is a response to Gettier's argument that a JTB is not sufficient for knowledge; it focuses on strengthening the 'justification' condition. Unlike RELIABILISM, virtue epistemology does not look at the way the individual has justified their belief on this *particular occasion*, but instead it considers the individual *themselves*.

Some people are skilled at archery because they possess the physical virtues of having a good aim, being strong, focused, and so on. If we put a skilled archer into an archery competition, we can be confident that they will hit the target.

Other people are skilled at knowing because they possess epistemic virtues – intellectual abilities which make them good at finding things out and justifying their beliefs. If we put someone with epistemic virtue into a situation where they must find something out, we can be confident that they will obtain knowledge. (A VIRTUE is a positive character trait, and EPISTEMOLOGY is the study of knowledge.)

A person with epistemic virtue does not believe everything they see and hear, and they treat information from some sources with a degree of suspicion; for example, they fact-check things they see on *YouTube*.

Reliabilist virtue epistemology	**Responsibilist virtue epistemology**
Focuses on the *abilities* of the individual, such as how good his eyesight and memory are, and how intelligent he is.	Focuses on the *character traits* of the individual, such as how much she cares about the truth, how open-minded she is, and how tenacious she is at seeking knowledge.

This approach defines knowledge as:

S has knowledge if and only if:

- P is true
- S believes that P
- S possesses epistemic virtue

In other words, knowledge is a true belief held by a person who possesses epistemic virtue, and it is their virtue (rather than luck) which has led them to form their true belief. This can be written as V + T + B, where V (epistemic virtue) replaces justification held by someone without epistemic virtue.

Strengths

- The focus on the strengths of the knower seems useful; some people are indeed more likely to obtain knowledge because they are more capable than others to fact-check propositions and sort truth from falsity.

Criticisms

- Even someone who is a very skilled knower could make mistakes sometimes, and these instances can be hard to spot. Just as it is difficult to know whether a skilled archer hit the target because of a perfect aim, or because they a small gust of wind luckily blew the arrow to the centre of the target.

Criticisms

- How can we tell whether someone has epistemic virtue? If we base our judgement on how frequently the individual obtains true beliefs, then this is a CIRCULAR definition: they are a skilled knower because they're usually right, and they're usually right because they're a skilled knower.

Response: Perhaps when someone has epistemic virtue, they know they possess epistemic virtue (this is a fairly weak response).

- It is not clear whether virtue epistemology solves Gettier cases (or fake barn cases) – did Smith have epistemic virtue?

Truth-tracking

Overview

Key philosopher: Nozick

Nozick's TRUTH-TRACKING theory is a response to Gettier's argument that a JTB is not sufficient for knowledge; it adds another condition to the JTB definition. In doing this, Nozick makes reference to POSSIBLE WORLDS (imaginary universes). The theory is that if someone would still have the same belief even in a (possible) world where it wasn't true, then it cannot be classed as knowledge.

This approach defines knowledge as:

S has knowledge if and only if:

- P is true
- S believes that P
- S is justified in believing that P
- In the closest possible world where not-P, S would not believe that P

In other words, knowledge is a justified true belief where the individual would *only* believe P in a world where P is true. This can be written as J + T + B + TT, where TT means 'truth-tracking'.

To illustrate this, consider Gettier's example (see p32-33) where Smith (S) believes that the man who will get the job has 10 coins (P). We must consider whether he would *still* believe it in 'the closest possible world where not-P'. To do this, we must keep everything in the example the same, but vary a tiny detail so that Smith's belief turns out to be false.

For example, let us imagine a world where almost everything was the same as Smith and Jones' world: Smith formed his belief that the man who will get the job has 10 coins, because he'd seen Jones with 10 coins, and it seemed certain that Jones would get the job. The only difference is that in this new imaginary / possible world, Smith has 9 coins in his pocket rather than 10. We can call this new world 'the closest possible world where not-P' (i.e. it's *almost* the same as the original world, but it's not true that 'the man who will get the job has 10 coins', because Smith gets the job, and he only has 9 coins).

In this 'closest possible world where not-P', Smith would still believe that P. In other words, even in a world where the truth was different, Smith's belief would remain the same – because Smith would still believe that 'the man who will get the job has 10 coins' even though the man who got the job (Smith) only had 9 coins. This means that Smith's belief is not truth-tracking, and therefore Nozick would say that Smith does not *know* that 'the man who will get the job has 10 coins'.

Strengths	**Criticisms**
• Neither of the JTBs in Gettier's examples are truth-tracking, so Nozick's theory is able to show that they are not genuine knowledge: truth-tracking can solve both Gettier problems. • Truth-tracking also solves the fake barn problem, because it would say that Henry does not possess knowledge. The closest possible world where not-P would be one where the barn Henry looks at is a fake barn (like all the others), yet Henry would still continue to believe that it was real. Henry's belief is not truth-tracking, and thus it is not knowledge. (Philosophers don't want to call Henry's belief knowledge, and so a theory which can show that it is not knowledge, is a good theory).	• It may not always be clear what an agent would have believed in the closest possible world where not-P. • It may be difficult to conceive of possible worlds; this is particularly problematic when we think of big changes. For example if P is that 'the Nazis lost WW2', then what is the closest possible world where not-P? It seems almost impossible to conceive of a world which would be just like our world, except that the Nazis had won WW2 (the differences between such a possible world and our world would be too numerous to conceive of).

Theories of Perception

Overview

Theories of perception attempt to explain the ways in which we perceive the world. We experience perceptions of everyday objects such as books, tables, houses, trees and so on – but how accurate are these perceptions, and do our perceptions really demonstrate that the EXTERNAL WORLD exists?

Immediate objects of perception

The phrase 'immediate objects of perception' means the things which we perceive directly (and accurately). The three theories of perception differ in what they say our immediate objects of perception are:

- *Direct realism*: the external world itself
- *Indirect realism*: sense data, caused by the external world itself
- *Idealism*: ideas

The falling tree

"If a tree falls in a forest and there is no one around to hear it, does it make a sound? Does it even exist?"

This old philosophical thought experiment is a useful way of differentiating between the theories of perception, as each theory has a different response to the question:

- *Direct realism* states that the tree exists and it makes a sound even if no one hears it.
- *Indirect realism* states that the tree exists and makes airwaves / vibrations, but since there is no one around whose eardrums can make sense of the vibrations as sounds, then the airwaves / vibrations cannot be called sounds.
- *Idealism* states that if no one (not even God) perceives the tree, then the tree does not exist. If God does perceive the tree but no humans are around, then Berkeley would probably say that it makes a sound. (Although it must be noted that God doesn't have eardrums, but he presumably has some other way of 'hearing' sounds.)

Direct Realism

Overview

DIRECT REALISM (also called NAÏVE REALISM by critics, or COMMON-SENSE REALISM by supporters) is a theory of perception which states that the immediate objects of perception are MIND-INDEPENDENT objects in the EXTERNAL WORLD. This simply means that everyday objects like cars and chairs really do exist, and our senses usually give us an accurate depiction of what the world is really like.

This is most people's notion of the world: if I see a green apple sat on a table, I assume that I'm having that sight experience because there really *is* a green apple sat on a table.

Properties of objects

Direct realists argue that an object's properties such as its size, colour, shape, taste, smell, and sound are an inherent part of the object – i.e. even if no one ever sees or eats an apple in a remote forest, the apple is still green and tangy and round.

Direct realists argue that we perceive objects directly without any intermediary. So when I see a red car driving towards me and I hear it honking its horn, I am sensing the car directly. I'm not just sensing my brain's interpretation of the car; I sense the car *itself*. Perception consists of just two elements: the object, and the perceiver.

According to direct realists, the world exists unperceived – in other words, if I leave the room, the apple and the table continue to exist with the same properties which they have when I look at them.

Strengths

- This is the common-sense everyday approach which people have about the EXTERNAL WORLD.
- In their normal lives outside of the classroom, even philosophers who criticise direct realism will (probably) still refer to colours, sounds tastes etc. as if they really exist.
- Direct realism maintains the appealing idea that objects continue to exist when I close my eyes e.g. my plant grows a little each day, and my house always looks the same as I left it, and the apple is still green even when I glance away from it.

Criticism

- Optical illusions are curious examples of how our sensory perceptions can play tricks on us. For example, there is no triangle here:

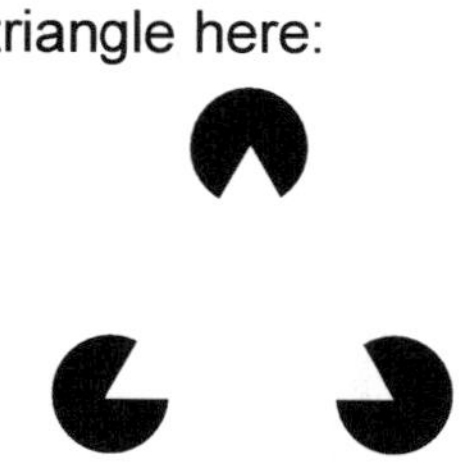

Other criticisms of direct realism are given below.

Criticism: Argument from illusion

The argument from illusion, put forward by Ayer, points out there can be a difference between the way things *appear*, and the way they *are* – this demonstrates that direct realism is false. This can be summarised as:

1. Direct realism states that we perceive the world directly and accurately
2. Sometimes things can *appear* to be different from the way they actually *are*:
    a) A straight rod half-submerged in water looks bent
    b) Circular objects appear elliptical when viewed from an angle
    c) Objects near to you appear bigger than objects further away
3. If things appear to be different from the way they actually are, then we do not perceive the world itself accurately; we perceive sense data

C. Therefore, direct realism is false

Responses

Direct realism attempts to respond to the cases in the argument from illusion:

- A straight rod in water appears bent because we are accurately perceiving light refraction
- Circular objects look elliptical because we are accurately perceiving the effects of foreshortening
- Closer things appear larger because we are accurately perceiving perspective

Nonetheless, philosophers such as Ayer argue that these responses are inadequate: if something appears a particular way (bent, elliptical, big, etc.) then if direct realism were true, then that would mean that there really were corresponding objects with those properties.

Criticism: Argument from perceptual variation

Russell looks at his table and notices that it reflects the light so that it appears to have a white patch on it – a patch which moves around the table as Russell moves around the room. Similarly, his table looks rectangular when viewed from above, but it can look like a parallelogram or a trapezium when viewed from different angles. Clearly the table isn't changing – it is just his perceptions that are changing.

Similarly, different people can view the same object and see different shapes and colours, or things can appear to vary in their colour depending on the time of day. Lukewarm water feels hot to someone who has just had an ice bath, but will feel cold to someone who has just got out of a hot jacuzzi. All of these variations in perceptions suggest that there is no 'real' or 'right' way to perceive the world.

The argument from perceptual variation can be summarised as:

1. Direct realism states that we perceive the world directly and accurately
2. My perception of an object such as a table varies as I move about the room (its colour, shape etc.)
3. The table itself is not changing its features
4. If things appear to be different from the way they actually are, then we do not perceive the world accurately

C. Therefore, direct realism is false

Response

A direct realist would maintain that we are directly aware of the table itself and the reflection of light cast upon it. The principles of perspective and optics can explain why the table appears to be different shapes when viewed from different angles; this demonstrates that we are accurately perceiving the table from each particular angle.

Criticism: Argument from hallucination

This argument points out that hallucinations (ILLUSORY PERCEPTIONS) are often qualitatively indistinguishable from VERIDICAL PERCEPTIONS (i.e. hallucinations look as realistic as real objects do). The argument can be summarised as:

1. Direct realism states that we perceive the world directly and accurately
2. In a hallucination, we perceive an object as having particular properties
3. The real object does not have these properties / no such object exists
4. If things appear to be different from the way they actually are, then we do not perceive the world accurately

C. Therefore, direct realism is false

Response

The direct realist can challenge premise 2: when we are hallucinating, we aren't *perceiving* anything: we are *imagining* it. A perception is a way of connecting with the world, whereas a hallucination is just our imagination (or problems with our vision processing faculties). So hallucinations don't challenge the direct realist standpoint.

Criticism: Time lag argument

This criticism of direct realism suggests that because it takes time for light to travel to our eyes, we never perceive things as they are at that exact moment in time. For an object right in front of you such as this book, the time it takes for the light to bounce off the book and into your eyes (and be processed by your brain) is infinitesimal.

However, the time-lag argument is most poignant when looking at stars. If you look at a star which is 10,000 light-years away, then the light has taken 10,000 years to reach your eyes. You are seeing it as it was 10,000 years ago: the star might not even exist any more! The time-lag argument can be summarised as:

1. Direct realism states that we perceive the external world directly, immediately and accurately
2. Light from stars and other distant objects takes so long to reach our eyes that we cannot see them as they are at the moment
3. If things appear to be different from the way they actually are, then we do not perceive the world directly and accurately

C. Therefore, direct realism is false

Response

Direct realists can respond that *how* we see and *what* we see are in fact the same sorts of things. Ask yourself: are you seeing a book, or light reflecting off a book? The direct realist maintains that these are different ways of phrasing the same event.

Similarly, we accurately perceive the light rays that are reaching our eyes now. Even if the star which the light came from no longer exists, we still perceive its light accurately as it is here and now.

Indirect Realism

Overview

Key philosopher: Locke

Indirect realism (also called representative realism) is a theory of perception which states that the immediate objects of perception are MIND-DEPENDENT (our sense data), but they represent and are caused by MIND-INDEPENDENT objects. Indirect realists argue that the external world exists, but we do not get a truly accurate picture of what it is like.

Primary and secondary qualities

Locke draws the distinction between primary and secondary qualities. He suggests that primary qualities appear the same to all observers, but secondary qualities vary according to the senses of the observer. This shows that direct realism is false, because some appearances are not true properties of the object, but rather, an ability of the observer.

Primary qualities	Secondary qualities
Objective qualities which are not dependent on the observer: • Size, shape, location, motion	Subjective qualities which are dependent on the observer: • Sound, colour, taste, smell

Consider an object such as a rose: I see it as red and I sense a particular smell; a dog is unable to see the redness, but his sense of smell is far greater than mine; a bee 'sees' the ultraviolet light from the rose; a bat knows the location of the rose using echolocation, but this doesn't give it any idea of colour. It would be arrogant and incoherent to assert that humans perceive the rose the way it *really* is, while all these other animals perceive it wrongly.

Criticism: Scepticism about the external world

If all we ever perceive are our sense data, and we can't ever experience the world directly, then we're trapped behind the VEIL OF PERCEPTION. This can lead us to SCEPTICISM about whether MIND-INDEPENDENT objects exist at all – perhaps the external world is an illusion.

Berkeley argues that we cannot know what mind-independent objects are like (or whether they exist) because all we have access to are mind-dependent objects (i.e. our sense data), and the two cannot be like one another. This means that there is no way to know whether our perceptions really are representing the external world.

Response from Locke	Response from Cockburn
We can't choose what to see: if something is in front of our (open) eyes, we just see it, whether we want to or not. Our sensory perceptions are completely involuntary (compare them to imaginary objects which we can voluntarily conjure up). This suggests that the external world is the cause of our perceptions.	Our sense experiences almost always agree with one another. For example, a person might simultaneously see a plate of food, smell it, taste it, and feel it; the fact that all these sensory perceptions agree with one another suggests that the external world is the cause of our perceptions.

Russell (like Locke) argues that the existence of the external world is the 'best hypothesis' (this is an INFERENCE TO THE BEST EXPLANATION, using ABDUCTIVE REASONING). Russell's argument doesn't *prove* the conclusion for certain; rather, the conclusion seems like the best explanation available. Such an argument can be summarised as:

1. We have perceptions which generally cohere with each other
2. We have perceptions which seem to cohere with other people's perceptions
3. We have perceptions which have continuity over time
4. Either we perceive the external world, or our perceptions are illusory

C. Therefore, the external world exists and we perceive it

Strengths	Criticisms
• Indirect realism improves on direct realism by responding to concerns about illusions and the ways in which our senses can deceive us. • The distinction between primary and secondary qualities seems to be plausible; secondary qualities really are dependent upon the senses of the perceiver. • The continuity of our perceptions (things remain where I left them, and plants grow over time) suggests that the world continues to exist unperceived.	• It seems counter-intuitive to say that an object is different from the sense data I receive about it; it really seems that I experience the colours and sounds from world itself, not just an impression of it. • If all I perceive are sense data then I am trapped behind the VEIL OF PERCEPTION so I can't be sure the external world exists (see previous page). • The external world is not the only possible explanation of our perceptions – it could be God, a dream, an evil demon, and so on. • Whilst indirect realism seems to fit in very well with EMPIRICISM (see p57), it seems that a lot of the things we learn through experience aren't 'real': colours, tastes, sounds and so on.

Idealism

Overview — **Key philosopher:** Berkeley

Idealism is a theory of perception which states that the immediate objects of perception are MIND-DEPENDENT objects (i.e. our ideas).

Berkeley's master argument

Berkeley argues that objects do not exist unperceived (he writes: "to be is to be perceived"); he suggests that an unexperienced object is as nonsensical as an unfelt pain.

This means that when an object is not being perceived, is ceases to exist. INDIRECT REALISM suggests that the only things we experience directly are ideas (i.e. sense data); Berkeley goes one step further and concludes that objects are simply ideas:

1. We perceive ordinary objects (tables, houses, etc.)
2. All of our perceptions are ideas

C. Therefore, ordinary objects are ideas

At this point, a critic might say it is counter-intuitive to suggest that objects flit in and out of existence as I close my eyes. The continuity of objects (things stay in the same place, grow a little each day, etc.) suggests that the real world *does* continue to exist unperceived.

Berkeley's response is that God perceives the world all the time and so objects *do* continue to exist when humans are not perceiving them – because God continues to perceive them.

Attack on primary / secondary qualities

Berkeley criticises Locke's distinction between PRIMARY AND SECONDARY QUALITIES, arguing that whatever sceptical tools we use to doubt the reality of secondary qualities, we can also use to doubt the reality of primary qualities. (For example, we now know that even 'solid' objects which are examined at the sub-atomic level actually consist of rather a lot of empty space, so perhaps 'solidity' is perceiver-dependent too.)

Furthermore, we cannot conceive of an object having a shape and size, but no colour. These arguments lead Berkeley to conclude that there is no distinction to be made between primary and secondary qualities.

Strengths	Criticisms
• It seems true that the only things we experience directly are our sense data. • As Descartes showed with his GLOBAL SCEPTICISM, it is LOGICALLY POSSIBLE that the external world does not exist, and my sense data are all part of a deception. • God solves the problem of perceptual continuity.	• Idealism struggles to explain how illusions and hallucination differ from VERIDICAL perceptions – if ideas are reality, then hallucinations are real. **Response**: God perceives the world all the time, so a hallucination differs from reality in that God does not perceive the hallucination.

Criticisms

- If ideas are all we perceive then idealism struggles to explain why a blind person has no idea of colour, whereas sighted people do – surely the reason is because sighted people see the real world, whereas blind people can only imagine what it looks like. This suggests that reality and ideas are different.
- Berkeley's master argument fails because it doesn't distinguish between IMMEDIATE (direct) and MEDIATE (indirect) perceptions. The premises of the argument (see grey box on p50) should say (1) We perceive ordinary objects mediately (2) All of our immediate perceptions are ideas. Once this distinction has been made, the idealist conclusion is not entailed.
- How can our ideas of pain, coldness, wetness etc. all be contained within the mind of God, when God cannot feel pain or have any sensations?

Response: The external world does not exist solely *in the mind of God*, it exists in reality, because it is perceived by God.

- Idealism can lead to SOLIPSISM (the belief that only I exist) because it distances us from the real world by suggesting that ideas are the only reality.

Response: This SLIPPERY SLOPE argument is unconvincing as idealism needn't lead to solipsism – I can agree that the only things I experience are my ideas, while still believing that other people experience their ideas.

- Invoking God to solve the problem of perceptual continuity is problematic. OCKHAM'S RAZOR suggests that if a phenomenon can be explained without invoking mystical beings, then that theory should be preferred. We can explain our perceptions by saying that they are representations of the real world (see indirect realism p47).

Types of Possibility and Truth

Overview

This is a detailed explanation of some key terms which you will need to be familiar with when studying EMPIRICISM and RATIONALISM (p57-68).

Possibility

An idea might be:

- Logically possible and actually possible
- Logically possible but actually impossible
- Logically impossible and actually impossible

It cannot be any other combination of these.

Logically possible	**Actually possible**
Something is logically possible if it can be imagined or conceived of; e.g. a flying donkey, a flying duck, or a man running a marathon in 10 seconds. Something which is logically possible might be actually possible, or it might be actually impossible.	'Actually possible' is our everyday use of the word 'possible', meaning it could happen in the world as we know it; e.g. a flying duck, or a man running a marathon in 3 hours. Anything which is actually possible is also logically possible.
Logically impossible	**Actually impossible**
Something is logically impossible if it cannot be imagined or conceived of; e.g. a 4-sided triangle, something existing and not existing at the same time, or 2 + 2 = 10. Anything which is logically impossible is also actually impossible.	'Actually impossible' is our everyday use of the word 'impossible', meaning it couldn't happen in the world as we know it, e.g. a flying donkey, or a 4-sided triangle. Something which is actually impossible might be logically possible, or it might be logically impossible.

Determining possibility

Logical possibility / impossibility is discoverable through rational reflection, DEDUCTION or INTUITION. (If we can conceive of it, it's logically possible; if we cannot conceive of it, it's logically impossible).

Actual possibility / impossibility is discoverable through experience. (If experience shows that it can be done, then it's actually possible; if experience shows it cannot be done, then it's actually impossible).

Examples:	Actually possible	Logically possible	Actually impossible	Logically impossible
A 5-sided square			Yes	Yes
X is green, but not green			Yes	Yes
Half man, half shark		Yes	Yes	
Jumping to the moon		Yes	Yes	
A green snake	Yes	Yes		
Jumping 3 metres	Yes	Yes		

Necessary and contingent

A proposition might be:

- necessarily true
- necessarily false
- contingently true
- contingently false

It cannot be more than one of these.

Necessarily true

A necessary truth is a proposition that must be true; it cannot be false (it's logically impossible for it to be false). Analytic truths and a priori truths are usually necessary truths, e.g. 'spinsters are unmarried women', '2 + 3 = 5'.

Contingently true

A contingent truth is a proposition which is true, but it could have been false (it's logically possible for it to have been false). Synthetic truths and a posteriori truths are usually contingent truths, e.g. 'Lego is made of plastic'.

Necessarily false

A proposition is necessarily false if it must be false; it cannot be true (it's logically impossible for it to be true, because it's a CONTRADICTION), e.g. 'spinsters are married men', '2 + 3 = 7'.

Contingently false

A proposition is contingently false if it is false, but it could have been true (it's logically possible for it to have been true), e.g. 'Lego is made of wood'.

Analytic and synthetic

A proposition might be:

- analytically true
- analytically false
- synthetically true
- synthetically false

It cannot be more than one of these.

Analytic	**Synthetic**
A proposition is analytic if you can determine its truth or falsity simply by knowing the meaning of the words (i.e. it's a definition). So 'red is a colour' and 'bachelors are unmarried' are analytically true, because they're true by definition. Whereas 'red is not a colour' and 'bachelors are married' are analytically false because they're false by definition. Analytic truths are necessary truths and are knowable a priori.	A proposition is synthetic if you cannot determine its truth or falsity simply by knowing the meaning of the words (i.e. it's not just a definition). So 'UK post boxes are red' is synthetically true, because it's true, but you couldn't know this from word meanings alone. Whereas 'UK post boxes are green' is synthetically false, because it's false, but you couldn't know this from word meanings alone. Synthetic truths are usually contingent truths, and are usually only knowable a posteriori.

A priori and a posteriori

A proposition might be:

- true a priori
- false a priori
- true a posteriori
- false a posteriori

It cannot be more than one of these.

A priori	**A posteriori**
A proposition is a priori if it can be known through reason alone. This includes mathematical propositions, analytic truths, necessary truths, and TAUTOLOGIES such as 'a frog is a frog'. 'Bachelors are unmarried' is true a priori, whereas 'Bachelors are married' is false a priori, because both are known through reason.	A proposition is a posteriori if it can only be known through experience. This includes almost all synthetic truths and contingent truths. 'Prince Charles is a bachelor' is false a posteriori, whereas 'Immanuel Kant was a bachelor' is true a posteriori, because these propositions can only be known through experience.

Unknown propositions

Generally, things which are not known or may never be known (e.g. whether aliens exist 10 billion light-years away) are synthetic, contingent and knowable a posteriori. This is because experience could, in theory, tell us whether they are true or false – it's just that we haven't gathered such evidence (yet). This is similar to saying that such propositions are VERIFIABLE IN PRINCIPLE (see p116-117).

Examples:	Necessarily...	Contingently...	Analytically...	Synthetically ...	... a priori	... a posteriori
Sharks eat fish		True		True		True
Rabbits eat fish		False		False		False
Vixens are female foxes	True		True		True	
Vixens are female cows	False		False		False	

Experience for a priori knowledge

Even if a proposition (e.g. 'triangles have 3 sides') is necessary, analytic and a priori, an individual still needs to have experienced language, numbers, and shapes to realise its truth – but this does not mean that the proposition is a posteriori. 'Triangles have 3 sides' is knowable a priori because once a person understands the terms involved, it can be known through reason alone.

Furthermore, just because a proposition is necessary, analytic and a priori, this does not always mean that it is obvious: there will be many facts of these sorts that you do not know.

For example, you may not know that tetrapods are animals with four limbs, that a rhombicosidodecahedron is a 3D shape with 62 faces, or that 84,726 x 17 = 1,440,342, but all of these propositions are necessary and a priori, because they are true by definition, and could not be any other way – even if you're not aware of it.

Hume's Fork

Hume divided knowledge into two categories which he called 'relations of ideas' and 'matters of fact'. This is known as HUME'S FORK:

- RELATIONS OF IDEAS: propositions which are discoverable through reason – i.e. necessary, a priori, analytic truths.
- MATTERS OF FACT: propositions which are discoverable through experience – i.e. contingent, a posteriori, synthetic truths.

Sources of Knowledge

Overview

There are three main sources of knowledge:

Empiricism	Rationalism	Innate ideas
The view that we are born knowing nothing and all of our knowledge is derived from experience alone. We use our five senses to experience the world, we remember what we have experienced, and this becomes our knowledge.	The view that reason is the ultimate source of our knowledge. We can use INTUITION and DEDUCTION to discover knowledge.	Ideas that are within us all along (i.e. we've had them since birth or prior to birth). These may be explained by something supernatural such as God putting the ideas into us, or by an evolutionary explanation of in-built instincts.
	Often, rationalists believe that we possess some innate ideas.	

Divine revelation

Occasionally, divine revelation from God is said to be a fourth possible source of knowledge, although philosophers often consider this to be a type of experience if it happens during our lifetime, or innate knowledge if it happens to us before birth.

One example...

Because empiricists claim that all of our SUBSTANTIVE knowledge comes from experience, if rationalists or innatists can provide just one example of something substantive which can be known without experience, then empiricism has been disproven.

Empiricism

Overview

Key philosophers: Locke, Hume

Empiricism is the view that we are born knowing nothing – the mind at birth is a TABULA RASA (blank slate) – and all of our knowledge is acquired from experience alone. Aristotle is one of the earliest empiricists. He notes that we use our five senses to experience the world, and we remember what we have experienced, and this is the source of our knowledge. Empiricism opposes RATIONALISM / INNATISM.

Locke: sensation and reflection

While considering how we come to our knowledge of concepts, Locke distinguished between sensation and reflection:

- *Sensation*: things we perceive through the five senses.
- *Reflection*: the internal operations of the mind such as our thoughts, emotions and memories.

Hume: impressions and ideas

Hume notes that the things we remember or imagine are never as forceful or vivid as our immediate perceptions of the external world, and so he divides perceptions into three types:

- *Outward impressions*: our sensory experiences at the moment they are happening. E.g. if I stroke my dog, then I have the impression of the feel of his fur, and the sight of his brown and white face.
- *Inward impressions*: our feelings at the moment they are happening. E.g. when my dog dies, I have the inward impressions of grief and sadness.
- *Ideas*: memories / copies of impressions (either inward or outward); these are less vivid than impressions. E.g. years later, I can recall my dog's face and the feel of his fur, and I recall my grief, but my memories are less intense than the impressions were.

Simple and complex ideas

Both Locke and Hume divide concepts (which they call ideas) into simple and complex:

- *Simple idea*: a single quality on its own, e.g. the colour blue, or a fresh smell.
- *Complex idea*: something with multiple qualities such as a daffodil or a horse.

How we form complex ideas

Hume argues that we can form complex ideas by manipulating outward impressions (ideas) of things we have already experienced. We can do the following:

- augment an idea (make it bigger)
- diminish an idea (make it smaller)
- compound ideas (put two or more things together)
- transpose an idea (mentally move it to somewhere else)

In this way, I can imagine a giant dragon in space by considering an impression I have had of an iguana, I augment the idea it to make it bigger, compound it with the idea of wings I have seen on a bat, and then transpose it into space.

Hume thus argues that there can be no concepts without impressions (we cannot form ideas of something when we haven't experienced its constituent parts). For example, a congenitally blind person will have no concept of colour.

Meaningless concepts

Hume claims that if we have an idea which cannot be traced back to an impression we've had, then it is not a genuine idea at all, but an error; a meaningless concept. He reasons in the following way:

1. The mind at birth is a blank slate
2. All ideas come through experience

C. Therefore, anything which has not come through experience is meaningless

Hume gives some examples of meaningless concepts, which include:

- *God*: we've never experienced God. We've just constructed the idea by AUGMENTING ideas of goodness, wisdom and power (see p68-70 for contrasting views about God's existence).
- *Myself*: I have a series of perceptions, but there is nothing beyond these which is a single impression 'me'.
- *Morality*: I cannot see the rightness or wrongness of acts. Morality is just a feeling I have about what I see (see p116).
- *Causation*: I can see that event A (e.g. a brick hitting a window) is always followed by event B (the window smashing), but I have not seen cause and effect *themselves*.

Missing shade of blue

Hume's rule that 'we cannot form an idea of something we haven't experienced' has only one exception – the missing shade of blue:

Suppose a person has experienced a variety of different shades of blue – except one. Hume argues that the individual will be able to imagine the missing shade of blue by augmenting or diminishing the shades around it.

Criticism

If the missing shade of blue is an exception to Hume's rule, then surely this is not the only exception. Presumably there can be missing shades of other colours such as green or brown. If one sees red and blue, can one imagine purple? Can one imagine sounds higher pitched than they can hear, based on the sounds they have heard? Can there be a missing smell, texture or taste?

Response

One might argue that purple is formed by combining our ideas of red and blue. This response seems unsatisfactory, however, since many people – including those who have been sighted all their lives – are unaware that if you mix red and blue it makes purple. People conceive of purple as a concept in itself, rather than the mere combination of red and blue. It is not clear whether Hume could satisfactorily answer these issues.

Strength

- It certainly seems that almost all of our beliefs, concepts and knowledge comes from experience; newborn babies know almost nothing.

Response: *Almost* all is not sufficient to prove empiricism – *literally all* of our concepts must come from experience if empiricism is true

Criticisms

- As shown on p44-47, the senses (and our memory of what we have sensed) are not always accurate, and can mislead us.

Criticisms

- If Hume is right that any concepts which can't be traced back to any particular sense experience are meaningless, then we have a great many concepts which are meaningless, such as beauty, justice, outer space, the bottom of the Pacific Ocean, dinosaurs, echolocation, sub-atomic particles, the Big Bang, WW1. (Hume cannot respond that we've read about these things in books, as the same can be said of God and cause and effect.)

Criticisms

- Almost all animals are born with instinctive abilities e.g. the ability to return to their place of birth, build nests, care for their young, or sing particular songs. It seems bizarre to maintain that animals have innate ideas, but humans are blank slates.

Response: There may be a distinction between innate abilities (mere instincts), and innate knowledge.

- In addition to the criticisms given here, you should use the arguments for INNATISM and RATIONALISM (p60-68) to criticise empiricism.

Innatism

Overview | **Key philosophers:** Descartes, Socrates, Plato, Leibniz

INNATISM is the theory that some concepts exist in us prior to any experience (i.e. ideas which are within us at birth). This theory opposes the EMPIRICIST claim that all our concepts are derived from experience.

Most RATIONALISTS – who believe that the ultimate source of our ideas is reason and logic – also believe that innate ideas exist. Hardly any philosophers claim that *all* our ideas are innate, but even if there are only one or two innate ideas, this is sufficient to disprove the empiricist notion of the TABULA RASA.

Descartes

Maths and logic

Descartes claims that maths, logic, and geometric truths are innate. He notes that we can use our rationality to understand shapes, even if we have never seen them. He claims this demonstrates that understanding is based on reason rather than experience.

His argument can be summarised as:

1. I understand the idea of a chiliagon as a 1,000-sided shape
2. I understand the idea of a myriagon as a 10,000-sided shape; this is different from a chiliagon
3. I have never seen either shape
4. If I try to imagine a chiliagon and a myriagon, my imagination cannot differentiate between the two of them (the mental images look the same)
5. If I consider the shapes using my intellect, I understand that they are very different

C. Therefore, I can understand shapes using the intellect, but not the senses or imagination

God

Descartes puts forward several arguments for the existence of God (see p68-70). The TRADEMARK ARGUMENT suggests that the idea of God is innate: God places the idea of himself into people's minds prior to their birth, like a craftsman signs his work with a trademark.

Criticism

Hume argues that we can create the idea of God based on things we have experienced, such as love, fathers, power and so on (see p58).

Socrates and the slave boy

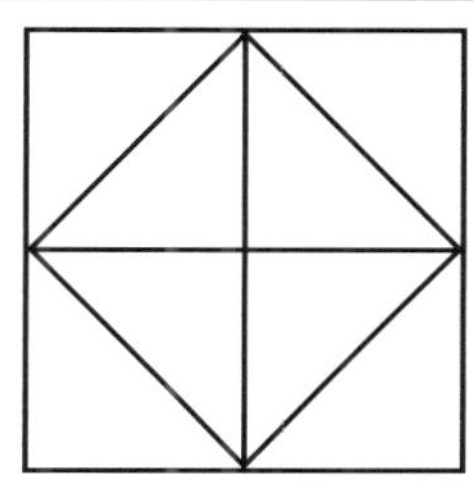

Plato wrote about a conversation which Socrates had with a slave boy, during which Socrates tried to demonstrate that knowledge of mathematics was innate. The questions were about how one could draw a square which has exactly half the area of an existing square (see diagram). The slave boy had had no education, but he got all the geometry questions correct; Socrates (and Plato) took this as proof that mathematical knowledge is innate.

Criticism

Socrates guided the slave boy in his answers, by asking leading questions such as "If it is two feet that way, and two feet this way, it would surely be twice two feet?" The slave boy's answers were very limited and mostly consisted of him saying "Yes". So Socrates' encounter with the slave boy does not prove that mathematics is innate.

Forms

Plato suggests that concepts we seemingly acquire on Earth are really just recollections from the world of the FORMS / UNIVERSALS – it contains universal perfect concepts such as 'goodness', and 'justice'. So knowledge of these concepts is innate.

Plato highlights his notion of the Forms with his ALLEGORY OF THE CAVE, which can be interpreted to mean that the things we see on Earth are but mere shadows, compared to the perfect Forms of such things. (We can see instances of beautiful paintings and beautiful people on Earth, but beauty *itself* only exists in the world of the Forms.)

Allegory of the cave

Several prisoners have been chained up in a cave their whole lives, such that they can only look in one direction. All they have ever seen are the shadows on the wall of the cave; to the prisoners, these shadows are reality. One day a prisoner escapes into the real world and is amazed by it; he realises that the shadows were mediocre copies of real objects. He tries to free the other prisoners, but they are confused, and prefer to stay watching the shadows, insisting that they are reality.

The mind as a block of marble

Leibniz argues that people have innate tendencies towards particular abilities. He draws the analogy of a veined block of marble: if a block of marble has veins in it which 'depict the shape of Hercules', then it is easier and more likely that it will be carved into the shape of Hercules. Similarly, children can have innate tendencies such mathematical or musical abilities. They do of course need to be exposed to numbers and musical instruments in order to cultivate these abilities, but the *tendencies* themselves are innate.

Language

Language acquisition is an ability which seems to be innate, and unlike other supposedly innate concepts, it doesn't rely on a supernatural explanation such as God. Instead, it can be explained via evolution (people who were able to learn language easily were more likely to survive and prosper).

Chomsky argues that infants' ability to learn grammatical rules quickly and easily is due to an innate concept of language. We learn the vocabulary and grammar of whatever language we are exposed to, but the *ability* to learn grammar without really trying seems innate.

Locke's criticisms of innatism

Locke criticises innatism, by arguing that if something was truly innate, then everyone would possess it, but since there is nothing which all humans (including babies) know, then there is no innate knowledge. His argument can be summarised as:

1. The principle "it is impossible for the same thing to be and not be at the same time" (the law of non-contradiction) is widely thought to be innate
2. Children and idiots* have no grasp of this principle
3. If there are some people who do not realise a principle, it is not innate
4. Therefore the law of non-contradiction is not innate
5. There are no concepts which every person possesses

C. Therefore, there are no innate concepts

Locke notes that all empiricists agree that the capacity for knowledge is innate. So if the innatists are only arguing that the capacity to realise such principles is innate but experience is needed to realise them, then innatism collapses entirely, for they are arguing the same thing as the empiricists!

Response

Innate knowledge does not need to be universal to be innate. Some people seem to have abilities which are impossible to explain by experience alone. For example, some people have the ability to know the day of the week of any date in history or the future – this hasn't been taught, but they just know it automatically. Even if only one person has some innate knowledge, that disproves empiricism.

Strengths	Criticisms
• There seem to be clear instances of people having abilities which are in-built from birth, such as musical or mathematical abilities. • Chomsky's claim about the capacity to learn language and grammar easily as a child is supported by good evidence – including that adults have lost this ability and find it much harder to learn a new language.	• In addition to the criticisms given here, you should use the arguments for EMPIRICISM (p57-59) to criticise innatism. • Mill argues that even an obvious mathematical truth such as 2 + 2 = 4 is learnt by youngsters through experience. They notice what happens when they have 2 sweeties and then they receive 2 more. They cannot know this without experience.

* By 'idiots' Locke means people with severe learning disabilities. At the time he was writing, 'idiot' was a medical term used to refer to such people, and it was not considered offensive.

Criticisms

- Innatism is unverifiable and unfalsifiable (it can't be proven either way) because once a child is old enough to answer questions, they have already had a wealth of experience.
- Children's ability to learn maths or language does not prove that they are innate: children can also learn how to use mobile phones, but it would be absurd to claim that this ability is innate – it's just an ability to learn.
- Descartes' and Plato's arguments rely on non-natural beings or places i.e. the existence of God and the world of the Forms. OCKHAM'S RAZOR tells us that if something (e.g. mathematical ability) can be explained without invoking non-natural and unfalsifiable things, then that is a better explanation. Empiricism can explain mathematical ability via experience, so should be favoured.

Rationalism: Intuition and Deduction

Overview

Key philosophers: Descartes, Leibniz

RATIONALISTS argue that not all knowledge comes from experience; instead, some knowledge can come through INNATE IDEAS (see above) and some comes through reason (intuition and deduction).

- *Intuition* is the ability to recognise the truth of a proposition simply by considering it.
- *Deduction* is the ability to work through an argument logically; usually this is from a set of premises to a conclusion which is logically ENTAILED by the premises.

Intuition is more than just a gut feeling about something. People might say things like: "I have an intuition that he's lying" but this is not a genuine intuition in the philosophical sense. An intuition is a way of recognising the truth of a proposition (perhaps because it's INFALLIBLE).

Deduction is not to be confused with INDUCTION and ABDUCTION, which both involve working from a set of premises towards a conclusion which is probably true, but is not logically entailed by the premises. Deductive arguments must always take a VALID FORM so that if the premises are true, the conclusion is guaranteed to be true.

The cogito

Descartes, through his GLOBAL SCEPTICISM (see p71-74), tries to doubt everything so as to find some beliefs which are certain. He considers the possibility that his entire life could be a trick by an evil demon. Descartes has the intuition that even though an evil demon could trick him about almost anything, there is one thing that Descartes can be certain about: his own existence. Even if he is a green ball of slime living in a tank somewhere, there is still something that is him, thinking at that moment.

Descartes' intuition is known as 'the cogito' because "cogito ergo sum" is Latin for "I think, therefore I am". The cogito is an intuition rather than something which is deduced from a series of premises, but it is laid out below along with his implied assumption that anything that thinks, exists.

1. I am certain that I am thinking (even if everything else around me is an illusion)
2. Anything that thinks, exists (implied)

C. Therefore, I can be certain that I exist

The cogito is said to be a SYNTHETIC A PRIORI proposition, because it is not a definition like ANALYTIC truths, but it is something that can be known intuitively through reason, without experience (a priori). Synthetic a priori truths are very rare indeed, and so the cogito is a small victory for the rationalists who wish to prove that SUBSTANTIVE knowledge can be obtained from reason alone.

Responses to the cogito

- Hume argues that it is possible for thoughts to exist without a thinker. Whilst this may seem implausible, Hume claims it is LOGICALLY POSSIBLE, so perhaps Descartes cannot be absolutely certain that he exists. Rather than saying "I think, therefore I am", perhaps Descartes should assert the more moderate "there are thoughts, therefore something exists".
- The cogito is very limited in its scope. Even if I can know a priori that I exist, it seems almost impossible to build any other beliefs on top of this foundation, to reach further knowledge. So the cogito is a rather meagre achievement.

Clear and distinct ideas

Descartes attempts to use deduction to reach his CLEAR AND DISTINCT RULE (that "everything which is clear and distinct is certain").

1. The cogito is certain 2. The cogito is clear and distinct C. Therefore, everything which is clear and distinct is certain	1. The cat is ginger 2. The cat is alive C. Therefore, everything which is alive is ginger

The problem with the reasoning behind Descartes' clear and distinct rule (left panel above) is that the SYLLOGISM is not VALID. This is because the premises can be true, but the conclusion can be false (the conclusion is not entailed by the premises). This can be seen by replacing the variables with other terms (right panel above).

By 'clear and distinct ideas', Descartes simply means anything which seems SELF-EVIDENT to him – i.e. an INTUITION. Descartes believes he has established that whatever is clear and distinct is certain, and so he believes that all of his intuitions will be true. However, as shown above, if the clear and distinct rule is flawed, then this does not guarantee the truth of his intuitions, and so any intuitions he has are dubious.

Deduction

Deduction is a more involved process than mere intuition, and it involves working through a series of premises to a conclusion which is certain. If deductive arguments are to be convincing, they need to take a VALID FORM so that the conclusion is logically entailed by the premises. The premises also need to be true, because any conclusion which is deduced from false or misleading premises is relatively worthless.

Here is an example of a deductive argument:

1. The angles within a triangle add up to 180°
2. Two right angles add up to 180°
3. Squares have four right angles
4. Four right angles add up to 360°

C. Therefore, the angles within a square add up to twice that of the angles within a triangle

Here we see that some known facts about triangles and squares can lead to a conclusion which one might not have realised before. But once one realises that the premises are true, the conclusion is self-evidently true.

All truths are necessary truths

Leibniz goes further than many other rationalists: he claims that every fact about the universe is NECESSARY, and can (in principle) be known a priori. Leibniz argues that God exists and is supremely perfect, and God has made this world the best possible world. This means that everything that happens is necessary – it cannot be any other way, because then it would not be God's perfect universe.

This means that in principle, all facts about the universe are knowable a priori, simply by working out what God would want the perfect world to be like. Unfortunately, our human minds are not advanced enough to work out these sorts of things, but still, says Leibniz, in principle everything is knowable a priori.

Criticism

If everything about the universe is knowable a priori, as Leibniz suggests, then we would know it. The fact that we don't know it is evidence that it's not knowable a priori.

Response

Mathematical truths are knowable a priori, such as the answer to 2,892,734 x 52,037,581 but our human minds are not (usually!) sophisticated enough to work this out by reason alone. There can be some things which are knowable a priori, but no human knows them.

Strengths

- There are some things which can be worked out by reason alone – such as mathematical truths.
- The cogito seems to be a genuine example of a SYNTHETIC A PRIORI proposition, which shows that substantive knowledge can be obtained through reason alone.

Criticisms

- Intuition is FALLIBLE: we can have mistaken intuitions even if they appear 'clear and distinct'.

Criticisms

- In addition to the criticisms given here, you can use some of the criticisms of INNATISM (63-64), and the arguments for EMPIRICISM (p57-59) to criticise rationalism.
- Deduction cannot tell us anything new; it only restates what was already contained within the premises in a slightly different way (such as the angles within a triangle and a square).

Criticisms

- Reason is learnt through experience: a baby cannot use reason to know propositions about angles within triangles or mathematical formulae.
- Deductive arguments often rely on premises which can only be known through experience – this means that the conclusion is reached through reason and experience combined.
- Empiricists argue that all knowledge which is derived through reason is not SUBSTANTIVE; it only gives us trivial truths. Necessary and analytic truths are just TAUTOLOGIES and definitions – knowing that the definition of a mermaid is part woman, part fish, does not tell us whether there are any mermaids in existence, so it's useless.

Arguments for the Existence of God

Overview

Key philosopher: Descartes

Descartes provides several DEDUCTIVE A PRIORI arguments intended to demonstrate the existence of God. It is worth remembering that even if all of Descartes' arguments fail to prove God exists, this does not mean God *doesn't* exist – it just means that Descartes hasn't proven it. These arguments and others like them are studied in more detail at A2.

Ontological argument

Ontological arguments for the existence of God rely on the definition of God, and assert that by definition, God must exist:

1. God is supremely perfect: he possesses all perfections
2. Not existing is an imperfection

C. Therefore, God exists

Criticisms

- Ontological arguments can define anything into existence: think of a perfect dragon, and not existing is an imperfection, so the perfect dragon must exist! (We resist this kind of SOPHISTRY for everything else, so we should resist it for God too).
- Kant argues that existence is not a PREDICATE (property) of something, and nor is it a perfection. Instead, an object needs to exist in order to have any predicates.

- Hume argues that all existential statements are SYNTHETIC, meaning that we cannot use reason alone to determine what exists. Reason might inform us that 'if x exists, it has property y' (e.g. if mermaids exist then they have fish tails; if God exists then he is perfect) but reason alone cannot tell us whether such things do indeed exist.

Trademark argument

The trademark argument involves Descartes questioning where his idea of God has originated from. His reasoning can be summarised as:

1. I am an imperfect being
2. I have the idea of a perfect, all-powerful God
3. The cause of something must be more real and more perfect than the effect (the causal adequacy principle)
4. Because I'm imperfect, I cannot be the cause of my idea of God
5. The idea of a perfect, all-powerful God must be caused by something which is actually perfect and all-powerful

C. Therefore a perfect, all-powerful God exists, and is the cause of my idea (he put the idea into me like the trademark of a craftsman)

Criticisms

- Hume shows that it is possible to form an idea of God by augmenting ideas we have experienced, such as love and power (see p58).
- There is no proof that the CAUSAL ADEQUACY PRINCIPLE is true.

Cosmological argument

Cosmological arguments focus on trying to establish the cause of something: typically they focus on the cause of the universe, but Descartes focuses on discovering the cause of his own existence. His reasoning can be summarised as:

1. Something is the cause of my existence
2. Either the cause of my existence is caused by something else, or it is uncaused
3. If it is caused by something else, then either that thing is caused by something else, or it is uncaused
4. There can be no infinite regress; instead, there will be an ultimate cause which is uncaused

C. Therefore, the ultimate cause of my existence is God

Criticisms

- If there can be an uncaused event, then why can't the Big Bang be the uncaused event? It doesn't need to be God who is uncaused.

- There can be an infinite regress: the pulsating universe theory suggests that there may have been big bangs and big crunches stretching back infinitely into the past.

Clear and distinct argument

Few – if any – other philosophers attempt to prove God's existence by clearly and distinctly conceiving it, but Descartes does:

1. The cogito is certain
2. The cogito is clear and distinct
3. Therefore, everything which is clear and distinct is certain
4. I clearly and distinctly conceive that God exists

C. Therefore, it is certain that God exists

Criticism

- Premise 3 – an INTERMEDIATE CONCLUSION – is not logically entailed by premises 1 and 2. Since the clear and distinct rule was reached via a SYLLOGISM which was not VALID, then the clear and distinct proof of God fails (see p65-66).

Proof of the External World

Overview

Key philosopher: Descartes

At the beginning of his '*Meditations*', Descartes engages in GLOBAL SCEPTICISM and doubts everything in order to find some beliefs which are certain. Once (he believes) he has established that God definitely exists (premise 1, below), Descartes attempts to prove that existence of the external world can be known A PRIORI, through DEDUCTION.

His reasoning about the external world can be summarised as:

1. A perfect God exists
2. A God who deceives is not perfect
3. Therefore, God is not a deceiver
4. I have perceptions of an apparent external world, which are vivid and seem real
5. If God is not a deceiver then perceptions which seem real, *are* real

C. Therefore, the external world exists

Criticisms

- Premise 1 can be criticised because none of Descartes' arguments for the existence of God are successful (see p68-70). We cannot deduce the existence of the external world from faulty premises.
- Descartes' original WAVES OF DOUBT (senses; dreaming; evil demon) can still occur even if there is a perfect, benevolent God. We know that our senses do deceive us (see p44-47) and dreams seem very real while they are happening. Also, given all the evil things which occur in the world which God does not prevent, we cannot assume that God would prevent an evil demon from tricking Descartes.

Hume's fork

HUME'S FORK divides knowledge into relations of ideas (analytic, necessary, a priori truths) and matters of fact (synthetic, contingent, a posteriori truths) (see p53-56). If Descartes is right, and the existence of the external world can be deduced a priori, then it would be an example of a synthetic a priori truth.

Synthetic a priori truths are very rare (they fit into *both* of Hume's categories of knowledge) and some philosophers argue that they do not exist at all. Hume argues that 'all existential statements are synthetic' to mean that we cannot use reason alone to determine what exists.

Limits of Knowledge: Scepticism

Overview

Key philosopher: Descartes

In everyday speech we use the word 'sceptical' to mean 'unconvinced'. We might say things like: "The Prime Minister has promised to improve the NHS, but I'm sceptical that this will happen". Philosophical SCEPTICISM is different from this: philosophical scepticism means suspending beliefs until they are proven to be true.

Incredulity and scepticism

Philosophical scepticism differs from ordinary INCREDULITY, because with ordinary incredulity, we doubt a particular fact or two, while maintaining confidence that our general picture of the world is correct.

For example, imagine you and I have just seen a person walk past: you believe it was George, but I believe it wasn't. This is type of doubt is ordinary incredulity, and there are practical ways of removing the doubt – for example, we can phone George and ask him where he is. We are not doubting our knowledge of the world *in general*; rather, we are both reasonably sure that we possess knowledge (I'm fairly sure it *isn't* George, whereas you're fairly sure it *is* George). Scepticism involves doubting knowledge *itself*.

Types of scepticism

Scepticism can be local or global:

- LOCAL SCEPTICISM: being sceptical about one particular area or field of study (e.g. doubting that we can attain knowledge about the nature of God).
- GLOBAL SCEPTICISM: being sceptical about *everything* (doubting that we can attain knowledge about *anything*, including reality, memories, and the senses).

The role of scepticism

Scepticism in philosophy (such as Descartes' scepticism) is used as a tool for finding knowledge which is certain. The technique is to suspend one's beliefs about everything, and then 'start from scratch' to see whether there is anything which can be known for certain.

Descartes' waves of doubt

Descartes uses global scepticism as a way of analysing which of his beliefs can be known for certain. To do this he has three 'waves of doubt' (each is an attempt at global scepticism, the third 'wave' being the most successful):

1. *Senses*: Descartes doubts his senses – the senses can be fooled and this gives us reasons not to trust them completely.
2. *Dreaming*: Descartes considers the possibility that his current experience could be a dream.
3. *Evil demon*: Descartes hypothesises that he could be being tricked by an evil demon, who has the power to make Descartes think that his life is reality, when in fact Descartes is something very different.

Responses to scepticism

It is worth noting that a sceptical position is not intended to be a philosopher's actual beliefs about the world; Descartes does not really believe that he is dreaming or being deceived by an evil demon.

Scepticism is just a tool for finding infallible beliefs. So we should not attempt a response to scepticism such as "Descartes is mad if he thinks there's an evil demon..."

Descartes' response to scepticism

Descartes, in his '*Meditations*', builds his beliefs up from FOUNDATIONAL BELIEFS (beliefs which are INFALLIBLE); one of these is the belief that God exists and is not a deceiver. Given this, God would not deceive Descartes about his senses and his life, and therefore Descartes concludes that he can in general trust his senses and that the world around him is not an illusion.

Rationalist response to scepticism

Descartes approaches his scepticism as any RATIONALIST would: he doubts his senses and experience, but he never doubts his ability to reason and make logical INFERENCES. The rationalist response to scepticism is to use reason to try to establish some foundational truths (infallible beliefs, which can be used as a 'firm base' onto which we can build other beliefs).

Theoretically, one can build up a system of infallible beliefs in this way. In practice, however, not a great deal of SUBSTANTIVE knowledge about the world can be obtained in this way. We might be able to know that dogs are canines (an ANALYTIC truth) but we can't know by reason alone whether any dogs actually *exist* (a SYNTHETIC truth).

Empiricist response to scepticism

Empiricists such as Locke and Russell place their confidence in experience (which comprises current information from the senses, and our memories of information from the senses). This means that the empiricists' response to scepticism is that we ought to trust our experience as being a genuine source of knowledge.

This is almost an INFERENCE OF THE BEST EXPLANATION (an ABDUCTIVE argument); empiricists suggest that given the competing possibilities that my experiences are wholly untrustworthy, or that they are largely trustworthy, the second possibility is the more likely of the two.

This isn't the strongest response to scepticism, since the sceptic is merely suggesting that we can't be *sure* our experiences are trustworthy. The empiricist seems to admit that we can't have *certainty*, but that we should trust them anyway.

Reliabilist response to scepticism

RELIABILISM is the theory that knowledge is a JUSTIFIED TRUE BELIEF where the justification is obtained using a reliable method (see p37-39). If, based on experience, we have found that a particular source of information is unreliable, then we should not trust information which we have obtained from it (and contrariwise, if a source has generally given us the truth, then we should trust it.)

Generally speaking, it seems as though our senses do give us reliable information about the world, and so the reliabilists are likely to suggest that we continue to trust our senses in general. As with the empiricist response to scepticism, this does not *prove* that our senses are reliable 100% of the time, but they are reliable enough to trust most of the time.

Moral Philosophy Overview

Normative ethics

- Utilitarianism – the right act is one which creates the greatest happiness for the greatest number of people:
  - Act utilitarianism – assess acts on a case-by-case basis
  - Rule utilitarianism – adhere to rules about what usually creates most happiness
  - Preference utilitarianism – satisfy most preferences
  - Other forms of utilitarianism
- Kantian ethics – the right act is one where the agent acts out of duty
- Virtue ethics – the right sort of life to lead is a virtuous life
- Similarities and differences between utilitarianism, Kantian ethics and virtue ethics

Applied ethics

- Eating animals – is it acceptable to eat animals?
- Simulated killing – is it acceptable to kill characters in computer games and other fictional settings?
- Lying – is it acceptable to lie?
- Stealing – is it acceptable to steal?

Meta ethics

- Moral naturalism – moral facts exist and are reducible to natural facts
- Moral non-naturalism – moral facts exist but are not reducible to natural facts
- Error theory – when we make moral statements we try to refer to moral facts, but no such moral facts exist
- Emotivism – when we make moral statements we are just expressing our emotions (boo-hurrah)
- Prescriptivism – when we make moral statements we are commanding others to act in a particular way

Moral Philosophy Basics

Normative ethics	Applied ethics	Meta ethics
NORMATIVE ETHICS is the study of what makes an action right or wrong. A normative moral theory is a system of ethics which tells people how to act – e.g. it will (ideally) show an agent which acts are right and which are wrong.	APPLIED ETHICS is the study of what is the right or wrong course of action in a particular situation or dilemma. It is also known as 'situational ethics'.	META ETHICS is the study of what people are doing when they make moral claims like "murder is wrong", and whether moral facts exist (i.e. whether it is a genuine fact or just an opinion that murder is wrong).

Consequentialist theories

A CONSEQUENTIALIST normative theory is one which focuses on the consequences as a way of determining which acts are right and which are wrong. Another term for this is a TELEOLOGICAL theory. Consequentialists believe that the end justifies the means.

For example, if Ronan gives 10 pence to charity, but Imogen gives £100, then a consequentialist would say that Imogen's act was more morally correct, as it created better consequences.

Deontological theories

A DEONTOLOGICAL normative theory is one which focuses on an agent fulfilling their moral duty – the consequences of the act are irrelevant. Deontologists see actions as right or wrong in themselves, and the end does not justify the means.

For example, if Jenny dives into a stormy sea to save Hanisha from drowning, but unfortunately both of them die, then a deontologist would say that Jenny did the right thing, even though two people dying is a worse consequence than if Jenny had done nothing.

Evaluating normative theories

You need to be able to evaluate normative moral theories. Some things to look out for are:

- Is there a CLEAR DECISION PROCEDURE? A clear decision procedure makes it easy for an agent to know what to do in a moral dilemma.

- Is it flexible or rigid? Does it take circumstances into account? We often feel that it is a strength of a theory if it can be flexible for different situations, but this may come at the expense of a clear decision procedure.
- Does it endorse horrific acts? We usually have the opinion that some things such as murder and torture are wrong. If a moral theory endorses these things, we find it troubling.

Classifications of acts

These terms are ways of referring to how morally good an act is:

- *Prohibited*: blameworthy acts which cannot be done (they are morally wrong) e.g. killing, stealing, torture, genocide.
- *Permissible*: neutral acts which are neither morally right nor wrong, e.g. eating a sandwich, painting a picture, talking to friends.
- *Obligatory*: possibly praiseworthy acts which must be done (they are morally right) e.g. telling the truth, caring for your children.
- *Supererogatory*: praiseworthy acts which go ‘above and beyond’ what is obligatory, e.g. running into a burning building to save a baby.

Relativism

RELATIVIST theories suggest that right and wrong vary across cultures, time periods and circumstances. For example, a relativist might say it’s acceptable – or right – to lie to a fat person who asks “do I look fat?” but it’s wrong for a politician to lie during an election campaign.

Strengths	Criticisms
• Relativist views are non-judgemental and accept the moral codes of all cultures. • It takes the circumstances of the situation into account and is flexible.	• It allows too much – if there is a culture where people torture children and execute rape victims for having sex outside of marriage, then a relativist would find it hard to condemn these things, as that moral code is ‘right’ in those cultures.

Absolutism

ABSOLUTIST theories suggest that some things are always right (or wrong) regardless of culture, circumstances and so on. For example, an absolutist might say that killing another human being is always wrong, regardless of circumstances (even in self-defence, as punishment, or as euthanasia); if killing is wrong, then it is always wrong.

Strengths	Criticisms
• Moral rules are clear and simple to apply – there is a clear decision procedure as the rules of morality never vary. • It allows us to make judgements of others simply and easily – e.g. we can know that a killer has done something wrong regardless of the circumstances.	• It does not take into account the circumstances of the situation – e.g. we intuitively feel that killing in self-defence is very different from killing for fun. • It's hard or impossible to know what the absolute moral laws are.

Ought implies can

Kant writes that 'ought' implies 'can'. This means that when we say that someone 'ought' to do something, we are implying that they are *able* to do it. It makes no sense to say "Faye ought to look after her daughter" if Faye is dead, or to say "Mohammed ought to donate 5 million pounds to charity" if Mohammed only possesses £1,000. Someone can only be morally compelled to do something that they are *able* to do.

Act Utilitarianism

Overview

Key philosopher: Bentham

Utilitarianism is a NORMATIVE MORAL THEORY which is CONSEQUENTIALIST, meaning the focus is on bringing about good consequences. It is a RELATIVIST theory because it suggests that a particular act – killing, for example – can be right in some situations but wrong in other situations. Bentham believes that happiness is the greatest good, and INTRINSICALLY VALUABLE; he refers to happiness as 'utility'.

Act utilitarianism states that:

The right act is one which maximises utility (produces the greatest happiness for the greatest number of people). This is the PRINCIPLE OF UTILITY.

Quantitative hedonistic utilitarianism

Bentham argues that if a person gets pleasure from push-pin (a simple children's game) rather than poetry, then he can choose push-pin, whereas if another person prefers poetry, then he can choose poetry.

In short, we ought to choose whatever gives the most pleasure, as this will maximise utility.

Egalitarianism

Utilitarianism is EGALITARIAN: a utilitarian considers everyone's pleasure in addition to their own. Each person's pleasure counts the same as everyone else – whether someone is a king or a homeless person.

The utility calculus

How can something as INCOMMENSURABLE as pleasure be calculated? Bentham put forward the UTILITY CALCULUS, which is a tool for calculating how much pleasure will be produced by an act. It measures pleasure in these seven ways:

- *Intensity* – will it be a strong, intense feeling?
- *Duration* – how long will it last?
- *Certainty* or *uncertainty* – how certain can we be that pleasure or pain will occur?
- *Propinquity* (remoteness in place or time) – how long will we have to wait for the pleasure?
- *Fecundity* (fruitfulness) – will the pleasure lead to more pleasure?
- *Purity* – will the pleasure eventually lead to pain?
- *Extent* – how many people will be affected by the decision?

For example, if Ryan is considering whether to buy his mum a necklace or some chocolates, he should calculate which act would produce the most (soonest, most intense, purest, etc.) pleasure according to the seven criteria, and that will tell him which present he should buy.

Strengths	Criticisms
• It fits with our general moral codes that doing something which makes people happy is a good thing to do, and doing something that upsets people is a bad thing to do. • Its EGALITARIAN nature makes it fair and objective; I shouldn't consider the happiness of one person as being more important than another.	• Utilitarianism suggests that we ought to be impartial and consider everyone's happiness equally, but in life we tend to value the happiness of our family and friends far more than that of strangers. • Human pleasure may not be the most important thing: it seems SPECIESIST (see p95-97) to only include humans in our calculations, and many problems with the world result from placing humans' desires above those of animals and the environment.

Strength

- It provides a clear DECISION PROCEDURE which is practical in situations where a small number of people will be affected.

Criticisms

- The utility calculus is an impractical tool for calculating happiness, particularly if considering large groups – e.g. a world leader considering whether to go to war could not possibly calculate the intensity, duration, certainty, propinquity, fecundity and purity of the pleasure / pain felt by the millions of citizens in the target country.

Response: It can be used as an approximate tool – e.g. the likelihood that happiness will be felt by people, and how far into the future they will feel it (weighed up against the pain and sadness they may feel for the duration of the short war).

Criticisms

- Utilitarianism ignores intentions – e.g. we generally regard a child who accidentally smashes 5 plates because they were trying to help tidy up, as morally better than a child who breaks 1 plate on purpose.

Response: The child with good intentions who broke 5 plates would increase happiness more than the child who broke 1 plate on purpose, so utilitarianism could say the child with good intentions was morally better, and they did the right act.

- There is a danger of TYRANNY OF THE MAJORITY – e.g. if 5 sadistic guards enjoy torturing a prisoner, then this is 'right' according to act utilitarianism, because the prisoner is in the minority and his unhappiness is outweighed by the majority (the 5 guards).

Criticism: Repugnant conclusion

Being solely concerned with the *quantity* of pleasure means that the "best" situation could be a massive world population. As long as people are feeling a tiny little bit of pleasure, it can outweigh the overall quantity of happiness of a smaller but happier population. Parfit called this the REPUGNANT CONCLUSION, as it does not seem appealing to have an enormous and minimally happy population, yet this is what QUANTITATIVE HEDONISTIC UTILITARIANISM promotes. Consider:

- 8 billion people each feeling 10 'units' of happiness = 80 billion units
- 15 billion people each feeling 7 'units' of happiness = 105 billion units
- 30 billion people each feeling 4 'units' of happiness = 120 billion units
- 65 billion people each feeling 2 'units' of happiness = 130 billion units

Criticism: Epistemic problem

It is not possible to know what is going to happen in the future, or what life would have been like if different events had occurred. If Robert murders a child, it seems like he hasn't maximised happiness, but how do we know that the child wouldn't have grown up to be a dictator responsible for the next Holocaust? If this is the case, then Robert has maximised happiness by ensuring that this never occurs. But there is no way to know this.

The effects of our acts continue indefinitely into the future, so it's not possible to know whether our acts today will maximise happiness in the future: this is the EPISTEMIC PROBLEM.

Rule Utilitarianism

Overview | **Key philosopher:** Mill

Rule utilitarianism is a NORMATIVE MORAL THEORY which arose as an improvement upon ACT UTILITARIANISM. It is a CONSEQUENTIALIST theory, but it does not focus on what the consequences of one specific act will be; rather, it focuses on what the consequences *usually* are for a general type of act. It is not strongly RELATIVIST, but nor is it an ABSOLUTIST theory.

Mill finds the endorsement of horrific acts (e.g. the sadistic guards – see previous page) morally objectionable, and he wishes to safeguard individual rights against such atrocities. He argues that even though an act of brutality might bring pleasure to several individuals, that does not make it a morally good act. Rather, it is evidence that they live in a 'sick' community rather than a healthy one.

Mill argues that the greatest happiness comes from individuals having freedom, but being prevented from harming others (e.g. by the law). He develops rule utilitarianism as a measure of the sorts of acts which generally produce pleasure. Rule utilitarianism states that:

The right act is one which conforms to a rule which (generally speaking) has been shown to produce the greatest happiness for the greatest number of people.

This means that a group of sadistic guards cannot torture a victim for fun, because generally speaking it does not promote the greatest happiness for people to live in a society where torture for fun takes place. So even if the act would create more happiness *in this instance*, it should not be done, because it does not conform to the rule which has been established over time.

Qualitative hedonistic utilitarianism

Mill focuses on the *quality* of pleasure rather than the *quantity*. He distinguishes between different types of pleasures, which he calls HIGHER PLEASURES and LOWER PLEASURES.

Higher pleasures	**Lower pleasures**
Pleasures of the mind, such as: • Philosophy • Highbrow literature • Intelligent conversation	Pleasures of the body, such as: • Food • Sex • Alcohol

Mill argues that once someone has experienced both types of pleasure, and become a COMPETENT JUDGE, they will choose even a small quantity of higher pleasures over a large quantity of lower pleasures (i.e. they will choose quality over quantity). Mill said:

"It is better to be a human dissatisfied than a pig satisfied"

"It is better to be Socrates dissatisfied than a fool satisfied"

By this he means that although pigs can experience bodily pleasures which come from food and sex, they cannot experience pleasures of the mind. This means that a pig's happiness is of an inferior quality to that of a human (even a dissatisfied human). The same argument can be made for fools, compared to philosophers.

Strengths	**Criticisms**
• Rule utilitarianism relies on the UNIVERSALISABILITY of actions, meaning that a moral agent cannot make an exception for himself or his particular case; this fits with most people's moral codes (we often say "if everyone acted like that, then the consequences would be terrible" as a reason against doing something).	• Not all pleasures fit neatly into the 'higher' or 'lower' pleasure category – e.g. eating caviar, doing yoga, doing a trivia crossword. • People will not always choose higher pleasures over lower pleasures – even philosophers will choose sex or pizza sometimes!

Strengths

- Rule utilitarianism does not endorse horrific acts which generally make people unhappy e.g. the sadistic guards.
- Focus on the quality of pleasure rather than the quantity allows rule utilitarianism to escape the REPUGNANT CONCLUSION.

Criticisms

- Some higher pleasures (e.g. learning philosophy) involve hard work and dedication, so they might involve frustration and struggling with concepts rather than pure 'pleasure' itself.
- If a society becomes particularly nasty so that generally, over time it is found that torturing disabled children does maximise happiness, then would rule utilitarianism have to endorse it?

Criticisms

- Rule utilitarianism does not seem truly utilitarian – if torturing prisoners would maximise happiness in this particular situation, then a theory which says the act would be wrong doesn't value happiness above all else. Rule utilitarianism seems to value other things (such as 'rights') more than maximising happiness.

Preference Utilitarianism

Overview

Key philosophers: Hare, Singer

Preference utilitarianism is a NORMATIVE MORAL THEORY which arose as an improvement upon ACT and RULE UTILITARIANISM. It is a non-HEDONISTIC form of utilitarianism, as it does not suggest that pleasure is the most important consideration when assessing moral acts; preferences are more important. (Act utilitarianism and rule utilitarianism are both hedonistic, as they place their emphasis on pleasure.)

People don't always prefer pleasure

Often, people's preferences will coincide with what they find pleasurable – but not always. For example:

- When Sophia gets a headache, she prefers not to take any medication for it; having the headache does not give her any pleasure, but she just prefers not to take painkillers.

- Joyce says that when she dies, she wants her ashes to be scattered in the Grand Canyon. Her relatives doing this won't give Joyce any pleasure (she'll be dead) but it will fulfil her preferences.

Preference utilitarianism states that:

The right act is one which satisfies the preferences of the greatest number of conscious beings.

Animals and foetuses

'Beings' means anyone or anything which is capable of conscious thought. Although it's not possible to outline an exact list of all animals which are included in this definition, it is likely to include almost all vertebrate animals, and some intelligent invertebrates such as octopuses and squid.

It is not always easy to know what the preferences of an animal may be. But it is reasonable to assume that being alive, having food and water, a place to live, the freedom to roam, and freedom from pain and illness are the sorts of preferences an animal would have.

Some philosophers argue that when weighing up preferences, we should include (human) embryos and foetuses as well as people who have been born. Other philosophers such as Singer argue that unborn embryos and foetuses should be excluded.

Nozick's experience machine

A criticism of act and rule utilitarianism is that pleasure might not be the most important thing to focus on when it comes to morality. Nozick puts forward the idea of an experience machine:

Imagine that there is a machine which can be programmed to give you any experience you would like, for the rest of your life. You have the option to enter the experience machine. Which of these situations would you prefer?

Option A:	**Option B:**
You enter the machine. You live the rest of your life feeling happy, believing that everything you experience is reality (but it isn't – it's an illusion generated by the machine).	You live your life in reality. Sometimes you will feel happy, but sometimes you won't – there's no way to know how your life will turn out. But at least it will be reality.

Given this choice, most people choose reality (option B), even though option A guarantees a life filled with happiness which feels totally real.

The fact that we would choose a mediocre reality over ILLUSORY pleasure suggests that we don't value happiness / pleasure as the highest good. It would seem wrong to force people into the machine, even though it would make them happy; instead, we should honour people's preferences, even if it doesn't maximise happiness.

Strengths	Criticisms
• Preference utilitarianism doesn't focus solely on pleasure – some things are more important than pleasure. • Both act and rule utilitarianism focus on maximising happiness for *people* – preference utilitarianism takes animals into account, even if they don't experience 'happiness'. • It encourages us to honour people's preferences even when they wouldn't know any different – e.g. if they are dead or they don't know that something is taking place, such as if your granny would prefer that you don't steal from her, even though she wouldn't notice if you did it.	• It's not always clear what people's preferences are – calculating preferences seems just as INCOMMENSURABLE as calculating happiness. • People's preferences aren't always in their best interest (a child might prefer not to go to school, but they should go, as it will be the best thing for them). • We often believe that human preferences are more important than animal preferences – e.g. chopping down a few trees to make my garden look nicer will satisfy my preferences, but not those of the birds and insects who live there, yet we still tend to view this as PERMISSIBLE rather than wrong.

Other forms of utilitarianism

Total utilitarianism

When calculating the potential happiness of an act, we should include the happiness of future people (and maybe future animals too). This is particularly relevant when considering having a disabled baby – we should consider how happy the baby will be. It is also relevant on issues such as climate change or the mass extinction of animals; we (currently living people) might not have to suffer the consequences of our actions, but future generations will.

Criticism

How many generations into the future must we consider? The consequences of our acts continue indefinitely into the future (this is the EPISTEMIC PROBLEM.) And can we really know how future people will feel about particular issues? People might be happy that the world's weather is unpredictable and that many dangerous animals are extinct.

Prior existence utilitarianism

This view opposes total utilitarianism. It suggests that when calculating the potential happiness of an act, we should just think about people (and maybe animals) who are alive right now. This avoids the epistemic problem of trying to calculate the happiness of our great-great-great-great-great-great-great grandchildren.

Criticism

It seems quite short-sighted and selfish to only consider our own happiness, but not that of future generations. Perhaps it is worth sacrificing a little bit of our own happiness (for example, by stopping using fossil fuels and not cutting down the rainforests) in order to secure a better world for our children and grandchildren.

Kantian Ethics

Overview

Key philosopher: Kant

Kantian ethics is a NORMATIVE MORAL THEORY which is DEONTOLOGICAL; it does not take the consequences of an act into consideration when evaluating its rightness. Instead, it suggests that performing one's moral duty is what makes an act right.

Kant aims to produce a moral theory which is as ABSOLUTIST as religious moral commands are (e.g. "Thou shalt not kill"), but his moral theory is SECULAR.

Hypothetical imperative

A HYPOTHETICAL IMPERATIVE is a command in the form of a CONDITIONAL (if-then) statement, such as:

- If you want to be slim, then you must stop eating so many cakes
- If you want to do well in your exams, then you must revise

With a hypothetical imperative, an agent can avoid doing the CONSEQUENT (the 'then' part of the statement) if they are unconcerned about the ANTECEDENT (the 'if' part of the statement). If you don't care about being slim, then you can eat all the cakes you want; if you don't care about doing well in your exams, then you needn't bother to revise. The imperative only applies to people who desire the antecedent – this means that the imperative only applies to some people or situations.

Categorical imperative

The CATEGORICAL IMPERATIVE is a (moral) command which must be obeyed all the time, by everyone, no matter what the situation is. Kant divides his categorical imperative into three FORMULATIONS (parts). You need to know the first and second formulations; the third formulation is simply a combination of the first two.

First formulation: universal law

Kant argues that it is morally wrong for an agent to make an exception for themselves. For any MAXIM (action) which the agent is intending to do, he must consider what would happen if everyone acted that way. Kant defines his first formulation as:

"Act only on that maxim through which you can at the same time will that it become a universal law"

The first formulation compels an agent to UNIVERSALISE any maxim he wishes to act on. If universalising the maxim would cause a contradiction, then the action is prohibited and the agent must not do it. Kant outlines two different types of contradiction:

Contradiction in conception / law of nature

This is a logical contradiction where it would be impossible for everyone to do X. An example is stealing: if everyone stole, then 'property' and 'ownership' would lose their meaning, and it would be impossible to steal in a world where 'property' and 'ownership' have no meaning. This shows us that we have a PERFECT DUTY not to steal.

Contradiction of the will

This is easiest to explain with an example: a maxim never to help others, when universalised, would result in the end that no one would ever help me. But I may require help one day (to become a better moral agent), and so it is a contradiction not to help others even though I will require help. A maxim never to help others would prevent us from becoming ideal moral agents – and that would be irrational (says Kant). This shows us that we have an IMPERFECT DUTY to help others.

Perfect duties	**Imperfect duties**
These are duties which apply all of the time. They are usually expressed 'negatively' such as "never kill" and "never steal". It is expected that we fulfil these duties; we do not deserve praise for not killing people!	These are duties which need to be fulfilled, but not all of the time; we have some choice over how and when to fulfil them. For example, you should help people in need, but you don't have to spend every second of your day helping people in need. When we fulfil imperfect duties, we deserve praise.

Second formulation

Kant argues that there is something special about human beings, and that people deserve respect and fair treatment merely because they are human beings. He states that it is wrong just to 'use' people as a means to an end; instead, you should always value them as a person as well. Kant defines his second formulation as:

"Act only on that maxim whereby you always treat humanity, whether in your own person or in the person of any other, never merely as a means to an end, but always at the same time as an end."

By this Kant means that it is acceptable to 'use' people as a means to an end, as long as you value them as a person at the same time. For example you use your teacher as a means to get a good exam result – this is fine, so long as you value them as a person too (e.g. by treating them with respect), and don't use them *solely* as a means to an end.

Aspects of Kantian ethics

The good will

It seems like there are many good things in life, like honour, love, justice, power, wisdom, and so on – but Kant suggests that any such quality can have a negative side to it. Doing an act out of honour, for example, isn't necessarily going to make it a *good* act; people sometimes kill for the sake of honour, which is clearly terrible.

Kant states that *only the good will is good without qualification*. By this he means that if something is done out of duty, and with good intentions, then that's what matters. The consequences of the act are unimportant; a good intention is INTRINSICALLY VALUABLE.

Acting in accordance with duty or acting out of duty

According to Kant, performing the right act is not enough to make our acts *truly* morally good; we must be acting for the right reason.

Suppose fathers have a duty to look after their children:

- Paul looks after his daughter, not out of duty, but because he loves her and cares about her.
- Mark looks after his daughter simply because he realises that it's his duty to do so.

Kant would say that because Mark is acting *out of duty*, he is doing the right act for the right reason, and this is the morally correct thing to do. Paul is acting *in accordance with duty*, but because he's doing it out of love and not out of duty, this is not morally correct (he's doing the right act, but for the wrong reason).

This is because our opinions and feelings can change (if Paul stops loving his daughter, he might stop looking after her) whereas someone acting out of duty (such as Mark) will continue to do their duty no matter what.

Strengths

- The focus on intentions is good (it avoids consequentialist problems of someone who accidentally brings about good consequences, but had bad intentions).
- It offers a clear decision procedure in a way that utilitarianism and virtue ethics do not; its ABSOLUTISM is a strength.
- It fits with our ideas about human rights, and the idea that no matter what a person is like, he still deserves a respectful level of treatment.

Criticisms

- Kant ignores the value of acting out of love, kindness and so on. (We generally think a father who only looks after his kids out of duty is not as morally good as one who acts out of love).
- The duty not to lie would mean that if an axe-man came and asked where your family were so that he could kill them, you'd have a duty to tell him the truth. (When presented with this issue, Kant was clear that you couldn't lie to the axe-man!) Consequentialists rightly object to this and state that the consequences of actions determine their moral value; a lie to prevent mass murder is a morally good act!
- There can be CONFLICTS OF DUTY: if Abdul promises to meet his friend at 12:00, but then he sees someone in need of help, he has a duty to help (but this would make him late), but also a duty not to break his promise.

Criticisms

- Kant gave very little consideration to the welfare of animals – a maxim such as "I will kick any pets which I own" passes both formulations; it can be universalised, and it doesn't treat any humans as a means to an end, but it doesn't seem very moral to act in such a way.
- Not all non-universalisable maxims are of a moral nature, e.g. the maxim "I will take a job as a web designer" is not possible to universalise, as there are not enough web designer jobs (people would be trying to get a job as a web designer in a world where there no were such vacancies). This is a contradiction, but surely it's not immoral to take a job as a web designer.

Prima facie duties

A problem for Kantian ethics is that sometimes there are clashing or competing duties. Ross goes some way towards solving this problem, by outlining seven prima facie duties (important duties which, other things being equal, we ought to follow). These are:

- Reparation (making things right when we have done something wrong)
- Non-maleficence (not harming others)
- Beneficence (kindness)
- Fidelity (keeping promises)
- Self-improvement
- Gratitude
- Justice

However, since Ross does not rank his prima facie duties in any particular order, it doesn't really solve the problem of clashing duties! Ross suggests that we need to use our INTUITION to know which duty to follow in a particular situation (see p111-113).

Foot's hypothetical imperatives

Foot argues that moral imperatives are not categorical, but hypothetical. This is because an AMORALIST can withdraw from the moral community, but still be perfectly rational (Kant equated morality with rationality, so this is a problem for him). Foot suggested that there are no moral rules which apply universally (categorically) but rather, that moral imperatives (even 'do not kill') are only right in some situations.

Virtue Ethics

Overview

Key philosopher: Aristotle

Virtue ethics is an AGENT-CENTRED NORMATIVE MORAL THEORY. This means that the theory focuses on what makes an AGENT morally good (or bad), rather than a particular act. (By contrast, Kantian ethics and utilitarianism are ACT-CENTRED MORAL THEORIES, because they focus on determining what makes a particular act right or wrong.)

Virtue ethics suggests that both the act itself and the feelings (intention) involved are important. It's not enough to save a child from drowning if your intention was to achieve bravery medals and adoration; the virtuous person would save the drowning child out of kindness and courage.

Eudaimonia

According to Aristotle, a moral agent's ultimate aim in life is (or should be) EUDAIMONIA, which means 'human flourishing'. This is more than just a state of happiness; rather, it is a state of moral, intellectual, spiritual and emotional wellbeing.

Function

The function of a bottle opener is to open bottles. There are different types of bottle opener, but a *good* bottle opener is one which opens a bottle well. In order to know what a good human being is, we must know what the function of a human being is – a good human being is one who fulfils the function. Aristotle suggests that the function of a human being is to be virtuous – he uses the Greek word 'arête' (which means virtue) – so a good human being is a virtuous one.

Virtues

Virtues are good character traits or dispositions which one possesses. Aristotle distinguishes between two types of virtues:

- *Intellectual virtues* such as knowledge, technical skill, intelligence and practical wisdom
- *Moral virtues* such as courage, temperance, modesty, and kindness

Habituation

The agent-centred nature of virtue ethics means that it focuses on the whole of a person's life, rather than a few particular acts. This means that the development of virtues is an important feature of virtue ethics.

Virtues are said to be developed through habituation (practice), much like the development of any skill such as playing a musical instrument or being adept at a martial art. Skills do not come instantly, and the process of practicing them is very important.

It also helps if an agent has a MORAL EXEMPLAR – someone who possesses virtues and can help the novice become more moral. The agent can aspire to be more like their exemplar, and when faced with a dilemma, they can think about what a virtuous agent such as their exemplar would do.

With practice over time, an agent develops PRACTICAL WISDOM – this is an essential virtue, which allows the agent to make decisions when faced with a moral dilemma.

Doctrine of the mean

How can an agent know which traits are virtuous? According to Aristotle, a virtue is the 'GOLDEN MEAN' (i.e. the mid-point) between two VICES. Vices are negative character traits.

Aristotle suggests that there are two types of vice: the vice of deficiency (when one lacks a particular virtue) and the vice of excess (when one has 'too much' of a particular virtue and they take it to an undesirable extreme). Aristotle states that extremes of a particular character trait are not ideal, and instead we should strive to have traits in moderation.

Here are some examples:

Vice of deficiency	Virtue (golden mean)	Vice of excess
Cowardice	Courage	Rashness
Feeling of inadequacy	Confidence	Arrogance
Apathy	Enthusiasm	Over-exuberance
Tight-fistedness	Generosity	Wastefulness

We can see that if one has too little courage, then he is cowardly, whereas if one has an excess of courage then he is rash – he rushes into dangerous situations without thinking it through. Thus courage is a virtuous trait and the golden mean, as it is the mid-point between the two vices.

Moral responsibility

Aristotle argues that we can only be held morally accountable (we can be blamed or praised) for VOLUNTARY acts. He suggests that two things may mean that our actions are not voluntary; force (this typically results in NON-VOLUNTARY acts), and ignorance – not knowing some relevant facts (this typically results in INVOLUNTARY acts).

Voluntary acts	Non-voluntary acts	Involuntary acts
Acts which are done knowingly and intentionally. E.g. you fire a gun at Jacqui's head (on purpose) and kill her.	Acts which are partially voluntary and partially involuntary. E.g. a dictator says that unless you shoot Jacqui, he will kill all your family; you only shoot her to save your family.	Acts where you are ignorant of what consequences will occur. E.g. you fire a gun at what you think is a mannequin, but it is actually a real woman, Jacqui, who dies.

Here we see that with the voluntary act, the desire to kill was present, while in the other two cases, the desire to kill wasn't truly present (in the non-voluntary case, you intend to shoot Jacqui, but you don't really *want* her to die – you're just killing her to avoid a worse consequence.)

In the involuntary case, when you discover that the mannequin was actually a real woman, Aristotle states that if you feel regret then the act was indeed involuntary, whereas if you don't care (or are happy!) that she's dead, then the act was non-voluntary.

Strengths	Criticisms
• The focus on feeling the right emotion in addition to doing the right act (that moral people enjoy being moral) is an improvement on Kantian ethics and utilitarianism. • The idea of habituation and a moral education seem important to a moral theory (we do not generally blame young children for 'immoral' acts, but as they mature, they are expected to develop morally); virtue ethics understands this.	• CIRCULARITY is a problem for virtue ethics, as when one asks 'what is the right act?' the response is 'whatever a virtuous person would do'; but when one asks 'what would a virtuous person do?' the response is 'the right act'. **Response:** A moral agent can emulate their moral exemplar, utilise the doctrine of the mean, and use their practical wisdom to know what to do.

Strengths

- The idea of judging a person's whole life rather than just a single action seems important.
- It is appealing to think that we can reach a state of eudaimonia by acting morally.

Criticisms

- It is not clear whether all moral acts contribute towards eudaimonia, e.g. having a pet dog and treating it well seems moral and is good for a particular individual – but is it really a moral act, and does it contribute towards eudaimonia? If we say yes, then surely all moral agents should have pet dogs; this seems bizarre.
- It has not been proven that eudaimonia exists; if it does exist, it is not certain that everyone desires it, nor whether a moral life is the only way to achieve it.

Criticisms

- Virtue ethics offers no clear DECISION PROCEDURE; it does not give agents clear advice on how to act.
- What is an agent to do when two virtues conflict or clash? For example, when someone is being offensive and threatening, the virtue of courage may suggest that I intervene, yet the virtue of temperance may suggest that I control myself; it's not clear which virtue should take precedence.
- It's not always clear where the mean lies between two vices, e.g. if filthiness is a vice of deficiency, and obsessive cleanliness is a vice of excess, then a medium amount of cleanliness is the virtue – but just how clean *is* the golden mean of cleanliness?

Similarities and Differences

UT = Utilitarianism KE = Kantian Ethics VE = Virtue ethics

Features unique to UT	Features unique to KE	Features unique to VE
• Primary focus on happiness • Different types	• Rationality and contradictions as a measure of rightness • Deontological nature	• Agent-centred moral theory • Focus on the whole of life • Aiming towards an ultimate goal (eudaimonia)

Similarities between UT and KE	Similarities between VE and UT	Similarities between KE and VE
• Act-centred moral theories • Rule UT and KE adhere to rules regardless of consequences	• Flexible to the situation • Rule UT and VE consider the usual outcome of acts	• Focus on intentions behind the act • Treat humans with respect simply because they're humans
Differences between UT and KE	**Differences between VE and UT**	**Differences between KE and VE**
• UT is consequentialist whereas KE is deontological • UT focuses on happiness whereas KE focuses on contradictions	• VE doesn't endorse horrific acts which bring happiness whereas act UT does • VE focuses on more than just happiness	• KE adheres to rules at all times whereas VE bends rules if judgement requires it • KE focuses on duty for the sake of duty

Eating animals

Overview

In the UK, most people eat animals; the most popular meats come from pigs, cows, sheep and chickens; cod, salmon, haddock and tuna are popular fish; prawns are also commonly eaten in the UK. Yet British people often consider the eating of other animals to be somehow morally wrong – horses, dogs, whales, monkeys, and so on.

Statistics: number of animal slaughters (for meat) per year across the world:

- Chickens: 46,000,000,000
- Ducks: 2,300,000,000
- Pigs: 1,200,000,000
- Rabbits: 850,000,000
- Sheep: 520,000,000
- Cows: 300,000,000

Given that most (if not all) of the animals we eat are capable of pain and suffering, many people argue that it is wrong to eat animals; our desire to eat them is the cause of their death, and it increases demand for meat, so that more animals will be killed. Given that humans do not *need* to eat animals to live a normal healthy life, it may be considered wrong to eat them.

Act utilitarianism

Act utilitarianism defines a right act as one which creates "the maximum happiness for the maximum number of *people*" i.e. animals do not feature in the calculation of happiness. If we do not count animals' emotions, then the question is simply whether eating meat makes humans happier than not eating meat. An act utilitarian might make the following argument:

1. It makes almost all people happy to eat meat
2. The right act is one which maximises happiness for the maximum number of people

C. Eating meat is right

However, Singer and others suggest that we ought to consider animals' happiness as well as humans' happiness (not to do so would be SPECIESIST). There is disagreement about the extent to which animals can feel happiness – but it is clear that the mammals and birds we most commonly eat can feel pain and fear.

So the question for utilitarians such as Singer is whether the total happiness generated by the people eating the animal is outweighed by the fear, pain and suffering of the animal which was slaughtered. This is not an easy calculation to make. Perhaps the way to maximise utility is for the animal to be treated well, killed painlessly, and then eaten.

Rule utilitarianism

Rule utilitarianism states that the right act is one which conforms to a rule that, generally speaking, maximises happiness for the maximum number of *people*. This means that rule utilitarianism (like act utilitarianism) does not appear to suggest that animals' happiness is worthy of consideration in any calculations of utility.

Mill claims that "it is better to be a human dissatisfied than a pig satisfied", so it seems as though Mill would not want animals included in any happiness calculations. This is because Mill believes that animals such as pigs can only experience LOWER PLEASURES. The problem for this type of argument is that some humans with mental impairments may only be capable of experiencing lower pleasures, but we generally say it's wrong to eat such people.

Preference utilitarianism

Singer writes that the key question when it comes to animal welfare is not "can they feel happiness?" but "can they suffer?" He argues that most animals can suffer (and they would prefer not to) and it is simple yet important to take animals' preferences into account when making utilitarian calculations. For example, a preference utilitarian might argue:

1. Almost all people prefer to eat meat
2. Animals prefer not to be mistreated
3. The right act is one which satisfies the preferences of the maximum number of beings

C. Eating meat is right if the animals aren't mistreated

Nonetheless, the issue remains that sometimes people's preferences might outweigh the animal's preferences. For example, some East Asian cultures prefer the animal to suffer prior to its death, believing that it improves the taste of the meat, and so animals such as dogs are often beaten, skinned and boiled alive. If this satisfies the preferences of 30 people who eat the dog, this outweighs the preferences of the dog. However, we would surely not want to call such brutality 'right'.

Kantian ethics

Kant's position on the treatment of animals is an interesting one. He argues that animals are mindless things, and so mistreating a pig is no different from 'mistreating' a rock.

Kant does, however, say that we shouldn't mistreat animals as it may turn us into the sort of person who might mistreat a human being. A Kantian ethicist might reason like this:

1. Eating animals can be universalised without contradiction, so it passes the first formulation of the categorical imperative
2. Eating animals does not involve treating any people as a means to an end, so it passes the second formulation of the categorical imperative
3. However, if someone enjoys mistreating animals, he might develop traits which cause him to mistreat people

C. Therefore, one can eat animals, but not mistreat them

Kant's SLIPPERY SLOPE argument does not seem convincing: most meat-eaters believe that it is acceptable to keep cows, pigs, sheep and chickens in unpleasant conditions, and then to kill and eat them. But only an infinitesimal number of people hold the view that it is acceptable to treat humans in a similar way.

A problem with Kant's argument is that although he discourages the mistreatment of animals, it seems to be for a strange reason. If farmed animals are kept in appalling conditions and killed in an unpleasant way, it seems very odd to object to this because we think that farmers may start treating humans in similar ways, or that people may start eating other people. Surely the reason why we shouldn't mistreat animals is because it hurts the animals *themselves*?

Virtue ethics

Aristotle's theory – like Kant's – distinguishes animals from humans due to their lack of reason and self-awareness, but this should not mean that mistreating animals is perfectly acceptable.

Virtue ethics places a strong emphasis on the habituation of character traits through practice, and so the virtue ethicist would consider what sort of character traits are being developed through the eating of animals. There seems to be little virtue in the eating of animals, but this doesn't mean it is *wrong* – it could simply be permissible.

Given that animals are thinking and feeling creatures, a virtue ethicist might argue that we should develop our virtue of compassion by treating animals well. Of course, it may be possible to treat animals well *and* eat them, but this is highly disputable. A virtue ethicist might reason like this:

1. The way to develop a character trait is through practice
2. Mistreating animals develops vices such as cruelty and violence
3. One should not engage in acts which develop vices
4. Eating meat can be done without mistreating animals

C. Eating meat is permissible but mistreating animals is not

Simulated Killing

Overview

Simulated killing involves pretending to kill people in unreal contexts, such as video games, theatre, and movies. NORMATIVE theories tend to condemn killing real people; but is it wrong to even *simulate* killing?

With movies, theatre, cartoons and television, the agent is merely watching the simulated killing, whereas with video gaming, the agent is performing the simulated killing themselves. These seem to present different issue; killing within video games is perhaps more morally objectionable because of the role of the agent in the killing (they are choosing to 'kill', rather than simply watching 'killing').

Objections to simulated killing typically come in two forms:

A. Simulated killing isn't wrong in itself, but it's wrong because it can lead to real violence / killing	B. Simulated killing is wrong in itself, regardless of whether it leads to real violence / killing

Argument A is a form of SLIPPERY SLOPE ARGUMENT because it suggests that a minor act (simulated killing) might lead onto major, more worrying acts such as real violence and killing. Clearly a response to this is that for the vast majority of cases, simulated killing doesn't lead on to real violence or killings.

Act utilitarianism

Being a CONSEQUENTIALIST and RELATIVIST theory, act utilitarianism cannot give us a definitive answer regarding whether simulated killing is wrong. Simulated killing is right is situations where it maximises happiness, and it is wrong in situations where it doesn't maximise happiness.

So if Greg enjoys simulated killing in video games (his happiness is increased), but he doesn't kill anyone in real life (which would lower overall happiness), then it is PERMISSIBLE or even right for him to play the games and simulate killing. The characters in the video games can't experience happiness, so they are not included in any calculations of utility.

The EPISTEMIC PROBLEM is an issue for act utilitarianism here: if Greg kills in video games 50 times a day for 30 years, and then commits a murder, how can we know whether the simulated killing played a part in causing him to commit murder? The acts which we do today may not seem to have immediate consequences, but the consequences may occur years down the line (or even generations down the line, if Greg tells his children how much he enjoyed simulated killing, then they kill).

So an act utilitarian either endorses simulated killing, or raises objection A against it, depending on the amount of happiness it creates.

Rule utilitarianism

Empirical evidence would seem to suggest that generally speaking, the vast majority of people are able to engage in (and enjoy) simulated killing without it leading on to real violence or killings, so the rule utilitarians would form a rule based on this:

1. Generally speaking, most people are able to engage in simulated killing without it leading on to real violence
2. Simulated killing increases happiness for many people
3. Therefore the rule 'allow people to engage in simulated killing' maximises happiness for the maximum number of people

C. Therefore, simulated killing is permissible

Kantian ethics

Kant's SLIPPERY SLOPE ARGUMENT regarding the treatment of animals can be used for the issue of simulated killing. Kant is unlikely to object to simulated killing itself (because it passes the categorical imperative), but he would probably point out that it can develop violent tendencies which could cause us to mistreat humans, just as mistreating animals could lead us to mistreating humans. Kant might argue like this:

1. Simulated killing can be universalised without contradiction, so it passes the first formulation of the categorical imperative
2. Simulated killing does not involve treating any (real) people as a means to an end, so it passes the second formulation of the categorical imperative
3. However, if someone enjoys simulated killing, he might develop traits which cause him to mistreat people

C. Therefore, one should not engage in simulated killing

For Kantians, the possibility that simulated killing may lead to real harm and violence (objection A) leads them to say that simulated killing is wrong for everyone, regardless of whether it leads to harm by that particular individual (a weaker form of objection B).

Virtue ethics

As with the treatment of animals, the virtue ethicist would consider what sort of character traits are being developed through engaging in simulated killing – virtue or vices? Engaging in simulated killing does not seem to be developing virtues such as tolerance, self-control or kindness, although it might, to a very limited extent, develop bravery.

On balance, it seems as though simulated killing develops more vices than virtues, and this means one should not engage in it. The virtue ethicist might reason like this:

1. The way to develop a character trait is through practice
2. Engaging in simulated killing develops vices such as cruelty, greed, anger and violence
3. One should not engage in acts which develop vices

C. Therefore, one should not engage in simulated killing

Lying

Overview

Lying is saying (or writing) a false statement. A more expansive definition of lying might include being evasive, exaggerating, or being 'economical with the truth'. For example if a 30-year-old describes themselves as 'young' then it is debatable as to whether this amounts to a lie. Because this grey area exists, in the exam, it is best to adhere to lies which are *clearly* acts of lying.

We often consider that there is a difference between a 'white lie' and a 'real lie'; if you wish to make this distinction in an essay, you would be wise to outline exactly what you mean by a 'white lie'. For example, a white lie might be defined as a lie which is told to spare someone's feelings or out of politeness, such as enthusiastically pretending to like a horrible birthday present you have received.

Act utilitarianism

Being a CONSEQUENTIALIST and RELATIVIST theory, act utilitarianism cannot give us a definitive answer regarding whether or not lying is wrong. Lying is right is situations where it maximises happiness, and it is wrong in situations where it doesn't maximise happiness.

An act utilitarian is likely to endorse 'white lies', for example suppose Andy goes to a lot of trouble to cook a romantic meal for his wife Sue. If the food is edible but not very nice then the way for Sue to maximise happiness is to lie and say that she really likes it.

Act utilitarians would be just as willing to endorse a 'real' lie if the consequences maximise happiness. For example suppose a politician falsifies records and lies to the UK public so as to win an election. If the politician then makes excellent decisions and is a better leader than the (honest) opposition would have been, then an act utilitarian would say that the lie led to the maximisation of happiness, so it was right.

Rule utilitarianism

In general, it does not maximise happiness when people lie, so rule utilitarianism would have a rule to this effect:

1. Generally speaking, it makes people happier to live in a world where people do not lie
2. Therefore the rule 'do not lie' maximises happiness for the maximum number of people.

C. Therefore, one should not lie

Weak rule utilitarianism

It might be useful to differentiate between weak rule utilitarianism and strong rule utilitarianism. The strong version would tell us that we should never lie in any situation (shown above).

However, the weaker version allows us to disregard this rule in some situations, or perhaps even to create a separate rule for 'white lie situations'. The rule could be based on the idea that although in general lying doesn't maximise happiness, telling a lie to spare someone's feeling *does* maximise happiness, and therefore it should be done.

Kantian ethics

For Kant, refraining from lying is a PERFECT DUTY (people should never lie). It fails the first formulation of the CATEGORICAL IMPERATIVE (and it usually fails the second formulation too) and therefore it is always wrong.

Because Kantian ethics is DEONTOLOGICAL and not CONSEQUENTIALIST, lying is wrong regardless of circumstances, so even if lying would bring about brilliant consequences, it should not be done. Kant's example of the axe murderer who asks the whereabouts of your family so he can kill them is a textbook example of this: Kant argues that you must not lie to the axe murderer. Kant argues like this:

1. An agent should act only in accordance with that maxim through which they can at the same time will that it become a universal law
2. Lying, when universalised, would mean that everyone lies
3. In a world where everyone lies, no one would believe anything anyone said
4. Lying is the telling of a falsehood (in order to be believed)
5. It would be a contradiction in conception to lie (and expect to be believed) in a world where nobody believes anyone

C. Therefore, one should not lie

Additionally, depending on the reason for the lie, it might fail the second formulation too. A 'white lie' which is told to spare someone's feelings might be said to be treating them as an end, whereas a 'real' lie is treating them as a means to an end. (But since lying has failed the first formulation, then an agent knows he cannot lie, regardless of whether his intentions are to treat others as a means or as an end.)

Virtue ethics

Virtue ethics considers what a virtuous person would do in the situation, and in this sense it is flexible to the situation. A 'white lie' to protect someone's feelings and make someone feel happy seems fairly virtuous, whereas a 'real' lie or a lie which is likely to hurt someone, is not virtuous.

Using the DOCTRINE OF THE MEAN, we can see that honesty is the 'golden mean' between two vices, but as noted above, there may be times when lying is actually the more virtuous thing to do.

Vice of deficiency	Virtue (golden mean)	Vice of excess
Lying	Honesty	Tactlessness

Stealing

Overview

Stealing is taking property that belongs to someone else (in UK law, it must be coupled with the intention to 'permanently deprive' the victim of the property in order to be classed as theft.) Theft is generally seen as wrong in the UK, because by law, we have the right to private property, and others do not have the right to deprive us of what is rightfully ours.

Act utilitarianism

Being a CONSEQUENTIALIST and RELATIVIST theory, act utilitarianism cannot give us a definitive answer regarding whether or not stealing is wrong. Stealing is right is situations where it maximises happiness, and it is wrong in situations where it doesn't maximise happiness.

So an agent needs to weigh up (using the UTILITY CALCULUS) how much happiness would be created by stealing, compared to not stealing, and then perform whichever action will create the most happiness.

Possible situations where stealing maximises happiness:	**Possible situations where stealing doesn't maximise happiness:**
• Stealing medicine from a large company to save someone's life. • Stealing when no one notices or cares.	• Stealing from those who have very little (e.g. homeless people). • Stealing which creates fear or distress among the victims (e.g. armed robbery).

Rule utilitarianism

Things are relatively straightforward for the rule utilitarian: generally speaking, it does not maximise utility when people steal. Often, the victim's distress at losing their property and the feeling of having been stolen from, outweighs the happiness of the thief. So the rule utilitarian would argue like this:

1. Generally speaking, stealing does not maximise happiness
2. Therefore the rule 'do not steal' maximises happiness for the maximum number of people.

C. Therefore, one should not steal

Kantian ethics

For Kant, refraining from stealing is a PERFECT DUTY (people should never steal). It fails the first formulation of the CATEGORICAL IMPERATIVE (and it almost always fails the second formulation too) and therefore it is always wrong.

Because Kantian ethics is DEONTOLOGICAL and not CONSEQUENTIALIST, stealing is wrong regardless of circumstances, so even if stealing would bring about wonderful consequences (e.g. stealing food to give to starving children), it should still not be done. Kant argues like this:

1. An agent should act only in accordance with that maxim through which they can at the same time will that it become a universal law
2. Stealing, when universalised, means everyone would steal property
3. In a world where everyone steals, the concepts of 'ownership' and 'property' lose their meaning
4. Stealing is the taking of other people's property (without consent)
5. It would be a contradiction in conception to steal other people's property in a world where 'ownership' and 'property' have lost their meaning

C. Therefore, one should not steal

Premise 3 states that if everyone steals then ownership of property loses its meaning. This is because if I steal something from you, then he steals it from me, but she steals it from him… then ownership becomes meaningless. We can't steal if owning property is meaningless.

Additionally, stealing almost always fails Kant's second formulation of the categorical imperative. (The only exception would perhaps be if one is stealing for the victim's own good – e.g. I steal the heroin my daughter had bought, to stop her from becoming addicted to it.) But these cases are very rare; in almost all cases, stealing fails the second formulation, so Kant would reason like this:

1. An agent should act only on that maxim whereby they always treat humanity never merely as a means to an end, but always at the same time as an end
2. Stealing is the taking of other people's property (without consent)
3. Taking people's property without their consent does not treat them as an end; it treats them solely as a means to an end

C. Therefore, one should not steal

Virtue ethics

The virtue ethicist must consider whether a virtuous agent would steal, and it would appear that generally speaking, being a thief is not a virtue one ought to cultivate. This is clear to us because stealing does not seem to be a virtuous mid-point in between two vices – rather, stealing seems to be a vice.

However, a virtuous agent should use his PRACTICAL WISDOM and take the circumstances into account. So in an extreme situation such as a famine in the aftermath of a hurricane, a virtuous agent might steal food from a supermarket in order to save lives.

Meta ethics

Overview

META ETHICS is the study of the nature of ethics – i.e. what ethics is. It encompasses theories regarding what we are doing when we make ethical statements like "Murder is wrong". (Are we trying to describe an objective moral reality? Are we trying to express our emotions?) It also involves the question of whether MORAL FACTS exist, or whether morals are simply opinions.

<table>
<tr><td colspan="5">Meta ethics:
What is the nature of ethical language?</td></tr>
<tr><td colspan="3">Cognitivism:
Moral statements articulate beliefs</td><td colspan="2">Non-cognitivism:
Moral statements do not articulate beliefs</td></tr>
<tr><td colspan="2" rowspan="2">Moral realism:
Moral statements are TRUTH-APT (can be true)</td><td colspan="3">Moral anti-realism:
Moral statements are…</td></tr>
<tr><td>false</td><td colspan="2">neither true nor false</td></tr>
<tr><td>Naturalism:
Moral facts are natural facts</td><td>Non-naturalism:
Moral facts are non-natural facts</td><td>Error theory:
Moral claims are all mistaken</td><td>Emotivism:
Moral claims express our emotions (boo-hurrah)</td><td>Prescriptivism:
Moral claims command others how to act</td></tr>
</table>

Cognitivism

Cognitivist theories state that when we make a moral statement like "murder is wrong" we are articulating our beliefs.

Moral realism

Moral realists believe that moral facts exist – i.e. that at least some moral statements are true. Often, realists see moral facts as MIND-INDEPENDENT (i.e. not just invented by people).

Non-cognitivism

Non-cognitivist theories state that when we make a moral statement like "murder is wrong" we are not articulating our beliefs – we are doing something else, like trying to influence others.

Moral anti-realism

Moral anti-realists believe that there are no MIND-INDEPENDENT moral facts.

The is-ought gap

Hume argues that “you can’t go from an ‘is’ to an ‘ought’”. This means that factual statements (‘the animal *is* in pain’) cannot entail a NORMATIVE conclusion (‘we *ought* not to hurt the animal’).

Also known as...

- Hume’s law
- Hume’s guillotine
- Fact-value distinction
- Naturalistic fallacy

This means that we could all agree on the facts, but disagree on the (moral) conclusion. Here is an example:

1. Animals feel pain

C. Therefore, you ought not to kill animals

Here the factual premise does not ENTAIL the value-based conclusion, since the premise can be true and the conclusion can be false. We’ve tried to jump from an ‘is’ to an ‘ought’. To make it a VALID argument, we would need to add another premise such as:

2. Killing causes pain

But still the premises don’t entail the conclusion, as we can agree to the premises but disagree with the conclusion. We’d need another premise to make it deductively valid, such as:

3. You ought not to do things which cause pain

This would make the argument deductively valid, but we have now put value-based (ought) premises into the argument. We haven’t bridged the gap between facts and values; we’ve just added values into the argument.

Hume states that there is no way that we can have a value-based conclusion which is logically entailed by wholly factual premises: this is the IS-OUGHT problem.

Argument from disagreement

It is clear that moral values vary widely across cultures and within them. Issues like abortion, sex outside of marriage, homosexuality, and which animals it is acceptable to eat divide opinion strongly. Some moral anti-realists use such disagreement as evidence that there are no moral facts – if there were moral facts, then why does everyone disagree?

Origins of moral principles

Our moral principles must have originated somewhere; philosophers disagree about the origin of our morals. Some possibilities are:

- *Reason:* our morals stem from our ability to think logically and rationally, and this enables us to grasp right and wrong, and to make moral judgements (Kantian ethics views morality in this way).
- *Emotions:* our morals are based on our emotions and experience; these help us to learn right from wrong and to make moral judgements based on how it makes ourselves or others feel (utilitarianism views morality in this way).
- *Evolution:* our morals are based on what helped our ancestors to survive and adapt (e.g. a society which kills babies would die out – we haven't died out, so 'don't kill babies' must be in-built into us).
- *Society:* our morals are learnt from society; we possess a moral code similar to others in the society we grow up in.

Mutual exclusivity?

When you are evaluating the meta ethical theories, it is worth considering whether they must be mutually exclusive, or whether it may be possible for two or more of them to be partially true. For example:

- Maybe when some people make moral statements, they are trying to describe a mind-independent moral reality (MORAL REALISM), but when other people make moral statements, they are expressing their emotions (EMOTIVISM), while a third group of people make moral statements to advise others how to act (PRESCRIPTIVISM).

Or perhaps some people are doing more than one thing at a time:

- Maybe when some people make moral statements, they are trying to describe a mind-independent moral reality (MORAL REALISM) *and* advise others how to act (PRESCRIPTIVISM).

Moral Naturalism

Overview | **Key philosophers:** Bentham, Mill, Aristotle

Moral naturalism is a COGNITIVIST, MORAL REALIST meta ethical theory. The theory suggests that when we make a moral statement such as "abortion is wrong" we are articulating our beliefs about a MIND-INDEPENDENT moral reality.

Natural facts

Naturalists argue that moral statements are propositions with truth-values, and just like non-moral propositions, they can be VERIFIED using evidence. For example, if I state: "there are 5 chairs in my house" this can be checked by looking around the house and counting them. Similarly, if I state: "murder is wrong" this too can be checked by looking at evidence.

Naturalists believe that moral statements can be verified or falsified using NATURAL FACTS. Natural facts are just regular facts about the world, like how many chairs there are in my house, how big the Earth is, what acts a person has performed, how much pain has been caused, whether other people were upset, and so on.

Reductionism

Moral naturalism is a form of ONTOLOGICAL REDUCTIONISM, because it suggests that concepts in one domain (moral properties of rightness) can be reduced without loss of meaning to concepts in another domain (natural facts). In other words, the rightness of an act can be discovered by examining the facts of the situation.

The question is: what natural facts should we examine when we wish to check how good an act is? Which natural facts are equivalent to goodness? Both utilitarianism and virtue ethics attempt to define goodness in terms of natural facts.

Utilitarianism

A naturalist might equate rightness (or goodness) with happiness, and say that the way to discover which act is right is to see which one produces the most happiness. If goodness is happiness then there is no mystery about which acts are good – we can just apply the principles of utilitarianism and that will show us which acts are good (see p78-83).

Mill equates happiness with goodness in this way:

1. If people desire something, it is desirable
2. Everyone desires his own happiness

C. Therefore, the happiness of everyone is desirable (it should be the goal of ethics)

Virtue ethics

Some philosophers suggest that Aristotle was a naturalist because his argument about function seems to describe 'goodness' in terms of natural facts (a human fulfilling their function and attaining EUDAIMONIA). However, it is not clear whether eudaimonia and the DOCTRINE OF THE MEAN are natural facts, or opinions (see p91-94).

Strengths

- We do seem to check the rightness of an act against the natural facts (e.g. if someone cuts a thing, we'll determine the rightness of the act by looking at the facts, such as whether the thing is alive, whether it can feel pain, whether there was good reason to cut it, whether it will make someone sad, etc.)
- We often seem to equate rightness with happiness, as the utilitarians suggest.

Criticisms

- Sidgwick argues that Mill commits the FALLACY OF COMPOSITION: Mill assumes that because everyone desires his *own* happiness, that 'the happiness of everyone' is a desirable thing.
- Mill commits the NATURALISTIC FALLACY by trying to bridge Hume's IS-OUGHT GAP; he moves from facts ('everyone desires happiness') to values ('happiness should be the goal of morality').

Criticisms

- There is disagreement about which natural facts equate to goodness – is it happiness? Is it fulfilling the function of a human being?
- Happiness is affected by our evolution (if we'd evolved differently, then killing might make us happy) and so happiness does not seem equivalent to a mind-independent moral fact.
- Moore posed his 'OPEN QUESTION ARGUMENT': there is nothing which is identical to goodness, because whatever a person says goodness is (e.g. happiness), we can still ask "but is happiness good?" and it is not a TAUTOLOGICAL question (see next page).
- The ARGUMENT FROM DISAGREEMENT (Mackie's 'argument from relativity') suggests that people disagree on morality because there aren't any mind-independent moral facts – just opinions.
- Ayer argues that moral assertions are not verifiable by examining the natural facts; he suggests that moral assertions are merely expressions of emotion.

Moral Non-naturalism

Overview

Key philosopher: Moore

Moral non-naturalism is a COGNITIVIST, MORAL REALIST meta ethical theory. It suggests that when we make a moral statement such as "rape is wrong" we are articulating our beliefs about a MIND-INDEPENDENT moral reality. Non-naturalists argue that although moral facts exist, they are not identical to (so cannot be reduced to) any NATURAL FACTS.

Instead, non-natural moral properties are seen as 'sui generis' (unique) entities, because they aren't like any other facts.

The naturalistic fallacy

Moore noticed that MORAL NATURALISM committed the NATURALISTIC FALLACY, and he posed non-naturalism as a response to this.

The naturalistic fallacy is committed when someone tries to move from factual statements like "the car hit the child" to value-based statements like "the driver ought to have driven more slowly" (it's a problem due to the IS-OUGHT gap). Non-naturalism doesn't commit the naturalistic fallacy, because it doesn't try to leap from facts to values.

Moore's open question

A closed question is one which is TAUTOLOGICAL, and shows that the person asking it doesn't really understand the concepts involved. For example: "I know you have a pet mouse, but is it an animal?" (Anyone who understands what a mouse is would know the answer to this question, so this is a closed question.)

Moral questions are OPEN QUESTIONS though, because whenever we define 'goodness' in terms of X, we can still ask "but is X good?" without it being a tautological question. For example, some people define goodness as happiness, but it is not a tautology to ask "but is happiness good?" So this remains an open question. Moore concludes that goodness is indefinable.

Intuitionism

Moore observes that we clearly possess moral knowledge, but how have we obtained this knowledge? Since non-naturalists such as Moore say we cannot reach moral facts by examining natural facts, then they need to suggest another way we can arrive at moral knowledge. INTUITIONISM is a theory which states that we can know moral facts via our intuition. (Most, but not all non-naturalists are intuitionists.)

What is an intuition?

Non-naturalists argue that a moral intuition is more than just a hunch or a feeling – it is the grasping of a SELF-EVIDENT truth. As with other A PRIORI truths, an intuition about morality might not be immediately obvious to everyone (not everyone realises that 68 x 72 = 4896, even though it is self-evident). This explains why different people have different ethical beliefs. Nevertheless, the non-naturalists argue that moral facts are self-evident and can be known via intuition.

Branches of intuitionism

- Moore claims that we have *general* intuitions about what is *good*. From there, we can work out the right act in a particular dilemma; the right act is the one which produces the greatest amount of goodness.
- Ross maintains that we have *general* intuitions about what is *right* (what our duties are). There are particular types of actions which are our duties (PRIMA FACIE duties such as keeping promises and not harming people – see p90). From there, we can work out the right act in a particular dilemma; the right act is one which conforms to our duties.
- Prichard suggests that we have *particular* intuitions about what is *right* (what our duty is). In each new dilemma, we have an intuition about our duty in that particular situation – we do not need to work it out from general intuitions of rightness or goodness.

Strengths

- Non-naturalism doesn't try to move from an 'is' to an 'ought', like naturalism does.
- Moore's open question argument seems correct, because however a person defines goodness, one can always question whether what they've said really *is* good.
- It seems true that moral codes are very much based on intuition – if a baby is drowning we intuitively know we ought to save it.

Criticisms

- Different people can have a range of intuitions, so intuitions don't seem to demonstrate what is right in a particular dilemma.
- Mackie poses the 'argument from relativity' (the ARGUMENT FROM DISAGREEMENT) which suggests that because people's moral views vary so greatly, this suggests that we do not have any moral knowledge, because no moral facts exist.

Strength

- Moore is right that moral facts and properties seem unlike natural facts and properties – moral facts can't be seen or checked in the same way that natural facts can.

Criticisms

- If Moore is correct that naturalism cannot bridge Hume's is-ought gap, then why should we believe that non-naturalism can bridge the gap? Non-naturalists are still attempting to move from intuition-based premises to ethical conclusions, which seems problematic.

Criticisms

- The fact that ethical dilemmas exist, where an individual does not know how they should act, shows that we don't always have intuitions about morality.
- Ayer's VERIFICATION PRINCIPLE (see p116) asserts that moral judgements are unverifiable and are therefore factually meaningless; they merely express emotions.
- Hume argues that moral judgements are not beliefs, because beliefs in themselves would not motivate us. This is similar to Mackie's argument from METAPHYSICAL QUEERNESS.

Error Theory

Overview | **Key philosopher:** Mackie

Error theory is a COGNITIVIST, MORAL ANTI-REALIST meta ethical theory. Mackie suggests that when we make a moral statement such as "torture is wrong" we are *trying* to map out a MIND-INDEPENDENT moral reality – but no such reality exists, and so all such moral assertions are false. So "torture is wrong" is false; "torture is right" is false; "giving to charity is good" is false; "giving to charity is bad" is false. All moral assertions are making a mistake.

Error theory differs from the other meta ethical theories studied at A-Level because it is both cognitivist and anti-realist. (With the other meta ethical theories, the COGNITIVIST theories are MORAL REALIST, whereas the NON-COGNITIVIST theories are MORAL ANTI-REALIST.)

Error theorists are not arguing that *all* statements about morality are false – for example, an error theorist would agree that moral statements such as "Poppy said abortion is wrong", "Keith is a rapist", and "It is against the law to murder" can be true. It is merely moral *assertions* such as "abortion is wrong" which are all falsehoods.

Queerness

Mackie uses the term 'queerness' to mean 'strangeness'. He argues that if moral facts existed, then they would be totally different from other types of facts in the universe, and very queer (strange). He outlines two types of queerness:

Metaphysical queerness

METAPHYSICS is the study of what exists, and what such things are like. Mackie suggests that if moral facts existed, they would be mind-independent and 'part of the fabric of the universe'. It would be very strange if the rightness of eating meat or the wrongness of abortion existed as part of the universe.

Also, moral facts would be motivating (if something is good, we would want to do it). This would mean that moral facts would have 'to be pursued-ness' built into them. Both of these factors would make moral facts metaphysically queer.

Epistemological queerness

EPISTEMOLOGY is the study of knowledge and how things can be known. Mackie asks the question: if moral facts existed, then how could they be known?

Other types of facts can be known either through experience or through reason (see p57-68), but Mackie states that moral facts cannot be known in either of these ways.

They can't be known through experience because examining facts will not show us the rightness or wrongness of actions (the IS-OUGHT GAP). And reason or intuition could not show us moral facts, because moral facts have no way of making themselves known to us; they are not self-evident. This makes them epistemologically queer.

God

Error theory is most convincing to a SECULAR mindset, because the two types of queerness which Mackie outlines do not seem quite as strange if God exists.

God would be able to 'weave moral facts into the fabric of the universe', so this would offer a (partial) response to the metaphysical queerness.

Also, God would be able to make moral facts known to us either by DIVINE REVELATION, or by making humans' brains sophisticated enough to intuit the moral facts directly, so this would provide a response to the epistemological queerness.

If one wishes to avoid appealing to God (as OCKHAM'S RAZOR suggests we should) then Mackie's argument from queerness seems convincing.

Strengths

- Mackie's metaphysical queerness seems right: if moral facts exist, then they must be 'queer' and different from all other facts in the universe in order to motivate us.
- Mackie's epistemological queerness seems right: there seems no plausible way that non-physical moral facts could make themselves known to us.
- Mackie seems right that when most people make moral statements, they aren't just expressing emotions; they really believe they are describing a moral reality.

Criticisms

- Epistemological queerness is not wholly convincing: it certainly seems that we do possess moral knowledge, as we can tell when a person does something immoral, such as raping a child. Perhaps moral facts can indeed be known through experience (NATURALISM) or intuition (NON-NATURALISM).

Criticisms

- If there is no moral reality in existence, then how can a moral statement be attempting to describe it? Non-cognitivism suggests that moral statements are just expressions of emotions or commands to others.
- It may be that moral facts are queer in the ways Mackie describes, but this doesn't mean that they do not exist. It is LOGICALLY POSSIBLE for moral facts to exist and be different from other facts in the universe; queerness is not disproof.
- Error theory doesn't seem to fully explain what we are doing when we make moral statements – surely we are doing more than just stating a falsehood? Error theory seems limited to arguing that the MORAL REALIST theories are wrong.
- It seems counter-intuitive to suggest that "murder is right" and "murder is wrong" are both false – surely if one is false, the other is true. Perhaps the statements have no TRUTH-VALUE at all because they are nonsense, much like the statements "tables are right" and "tables are wrong".

Emotivism

Overview

Key philosophers: Ayer, Vienna Circle, Hume

Emotivism is a NON-COGNITIVIST, MORAL ANTI-REALIST meta ethical theory. It suggests that when we make a moral statement such as "genocide is wrong" we are not articulating beliefs about a MIND-INDEPENDENT moral reality – rather, we are merely expressing our emotions.

Logical positivism

LOGICAL POSITIVISM is an approach towards philosophical topics which involves taking a very logical, analytical stance. It was popular in the early 20th century.

- The Vienna Circle were a group of logical positivists working together in Vienna, Austria
- Ayer was another logical positivist working independently

Both Ayer and the Vienna Circle assert the VERIFICATION PRINCIPLE as a criterion of meaning. In other words, the verification principle is a tool for showing which propositions are (factually) meaningful.

Verification principle

All ANALYTIC statements (such as "yellow is a colour") and TAUTOLOGIES (such as "yellow is yellow") are factually meaningful. But not all SYNTHETIC statements are meaningful; the verification principle states that in order for a synthetic proposition to be factually meaningful, it must be verifiable in principle and/or by sense experience. Propositions which are neither analytic nor verifiable (in principle) are factually meaningless.

The verification principle can be summarised as:

In order for a proposition to be factually meaningful, it must be either:

- Analytic ...or...
- Synthetic and verifiable (in principle)

'Verifiable in principle' means that it must be possible – LOGICALLY POSSIBLE at least – to check whether the claim is true. For example, the statement "there is a flip-flop on one of Jupiter's moons" is verifiable in principle because we know what could be done to verify the claim. Namely, we'd need to check the entire surface of each of Jupiter's moons, and the evidence we gathered would prove the claim to be true or false.

It can't be done *in practice* (yet), but we know what evidence it would take for it to be verified, so it is verifiable *in principle*. So the statement "there is a flip-flop on one of Jupiter's moons" is factually meaningful.

An ethical proposition such as "torture is wrong" is not true by definition, so it is not analytic. Nor is it verifiable in principle, because there are no facts which could prove the truth or falsity the proposition (due to Hume's IS-OUGHT gap, we cannot examine facts and arrive at a NORMATIVE / value-based conclusion.) This means that ethical propositions such as "torture is wrong" are not factually meaningful.

Factually meaningful

The logical positivists are not suggesting that "murder is wrong" is gibberish or that no one understands it – they are merely suggesting that "murder is wrong" is not *factually* meaningful. It is clear to Ayer and the Vienna Circle that moral statements carry meaning inasmuch as they express feelings or emotions, but they do not express TRUTH-APT propositions (they cannot be true or false).

Aesthetic statements such as "the Queen is beautiful" or poetic statements such as "love is a chamber teeming with fanged parasites" are meaningful as expressions of opinions, emotions or feelings, but they are not *factually* meaningful – they cannot be verified. The logical positivists argue that the same is true of an ethical statement such as "eating meat is wrong" – it expresses an emotion, but nothing more.

The Vienna circle's argument regarding the status of moral language is:

1. The only factually meaningful statements are analytic or verifiable (in principle)
2. Moral statements are not analytic
3. Moral statements are not verifiable in principle

C. Therefore, moral statements are factually meaningless. They merely express emotions

Boo-hurrah theory

Emotivism is nicknamed the BOO-HURRAH THEORY, because emotivists claim that a moral statement merely expresses one's emotions about something. So saying "genocide is wrong" and "protecting babies is right" is equivalent to saying "genocide: boo!" and "protecting babies: hurrah!"

Moral desires

Stevenson distinguishes between beliefs and desires. Beliefs are about how we think the world is (e.g. I have £1000 in the bank), whereas desires are about how we think the world should be or how we want it to be (e.g. I wish I was a millionaire). Beliefs are truth-apt whereas desires are just hopes, and do not have a TRUTH-VALUE – one cannot have a 'false desire'.

Stevenson argues that moral propositions are desires; saying "genocide is wrong" is the same as saying "I wish genocide didn't take place". Such a desire cannot be true or false – it is nothing more than an expression of hope, a wish, or emotion.

Strengths

- Emotivism explains (in a way that MORAL REALISM cannot) why moral judgements motivate us – namely because they carry emotional meanings from the speaker.
- It seems true that many moral debates are emotional ones, where people express strong emotions about the issue.
- Emotivism accounts for the ARGUMENT FROM DISAGREEMENT by showing that people all have different emotions about moral matters.

Criticisms

- Emotivism does not give adequate weight to moral deliberation and fact-gathering. If there is a moral issue about which you have little knowledge, then you will gather facts in order to make a reasoned moral judgement. Emotivism overlooks this rational side of morality and suggests that moral judgements are all emotional ones.

Criticisms

- The verification principle itself is not verifiable – we cannot check (even in principle) whether all synthetic non-verifiable statements are factually meaningless, so the verification principle is self-defeating.
- There are many types of language which express emotions or motivate us, e.g. poetry and advertising. Surely there is something more to moral statements than merely an expression of emotions?
- Emotivism oversimplifies moral language to boo-hurrah statements. Morality seems to be more than just people expressing their emotions: moral discussions are much more heated than e.g. a discussion about whether broccoli is delicious.

Criticisms

- Ethical language isn't always expressing emotions; one can calmly say that they believe euthanasia is permissible without being emotional about it; it seems as though such people are articulating beliefs (as COGNITIVISM suggests).

Response: The primary purpose of moral language is emotive, even if it can be used for other purposes.

- Moral facts might be ESCHATOLOGICALLY VERIFIABLE (verifiable after death). It is possible that when we die we will experience an afterlife where God makes the truths about morality clear to us; thus we can envisage how a moral statement could be verified in principle.
- The logical positivists don't adequately demonstrate why we ought to subscribe to the verification principle: why does something need to be verifiable in order to be factually meaningful?
- Reducing morality to mere emotions means that we can't say that an abhorrent act such as child abuse is wrong – all we can say is that we dislike it ("boo to child abuse!") Thus emotivism can collapse into MORAL NIHILISM (the belief that nothing is morally wrong).
- It may be possible to bridge the is-ought gap as the MORAL NATURALISTS suggest – perhaps fact-gathering about torture can demonstrate the wrongness of it. If so, then moral statements are synthetic and verifiable – and therefore they are meaningful according to the verification principle.
- In the UK, people used to think it was normal and acceptable for a man to rape and beat his wife; we don't think this any more. This seems like MORAL PROGRESS – but emotivism cannot view it as moral progress, because moral anti-realists are committed to the idea that there is no mind-independent moral reality. This means that medieval morality is no better or worse than our present day morality, because we are no closer to understanding moral facts – because there are no moral facts.

Prescriptivism

Overview

Key philosopher: Hare

Prescriptivism is a NON-COGNITIVIST, MORAL ANTI-REALIST meta ethical theory. Prescriptivists argue that when we make a moral statement such as "cannibalism is wrong" we are not articulating beliefs about a MIND-INDEPENDENT moral reality – rather, we are commanding others how to act (i.e. "do not be a cannibal").

Commanding actions

An IMPERATIVE is a command; imperatives can be explicit (such as "come here now") or implicit (such as "it would be good if you came here now"). We clearly understand that the second sort of statement means something very similar to the first command – albeit more subtle. Moral statements such as "infanticide is wrong" are the second type of (implicit) imperative. The statement provides guidance for you about how I think you ought to act.

Note that an imperative is not an attempt to persuade – persuasion may take a lot more effort and require evidence and reasons. Notice the difference between "don't eat meat" (a prescription / command) and "you shouldn't eat meat because farmed mammals are highly intelligent, they suffer pain and misery during their lives, and their slaughter is brutal…" and so on (an attempt to persuade).

Commending actions

We use the word 'good' to commend (praise) something.

When I say "that's a good pizza" I am praising it. Perhaps I think it's good because of the flavour of the toppings and the crispness of the base, but I'm not only describing the features of the pizza. My judgement of the pizza is based on its features, but when I call it 'good' I'm primarily commending it.	When I say "Elliot is a good person" I am praising him. Perhaps I think he's good because of his bravery and generosity, but I'm not only describing his personality traits. My judgement of Elliot is based on his personality, but when I call him 'good' I'm primarily commending him.

We often believe that we can judge what counts as a good person – but standards are not universal; they vary between individuals and cultures, rather than being true or false.

You may think that a man who never gives money to charity can still be a good person, while I may think he cannot. This means that a moral assertion such as "giving money to charity is right" is not TRUTH-APT – I am simply commending those who give to charity, and I am also commanding you to give money to charity.

Universalisability

Hare argues that we must be willing to UNIVERSALISE our moral commands, and not make an exception for ourselves. For example if I maintain it is wrong for people to punch me, then I must also maintain it is wrong for me to punch other people – to think otherwise is contradictory (unless there is some relevant difference between the two cases). In this way Hare's prescriptivism shares some features with KANTIAN ETHICS.

However, Hare's prescriptivism is not focused on logical contradictions, but merely on the opinions and preferences of the moral agent. It is very similar to the GOLDEN RULE of Christianity: 'do unto others as you would have others do unto you'. This is another way of saying treat other people as you want to be treated.

Strengths

- It does seem that when we make moral statements, we are trying to influence others; we want others to act the way we deem to be moral.
- The word 'good' is indeed used to commend people or acts, and to command others with phrases like "it would be good if you stopped taking drugs".

Criticisms

- Reducing morality to just commending and commanding means that we can't say that an abhorrent act such as mass murder is wrong – all we can say is "don't commit mass murder". Thus prescriptivism can collapse into MORAL NIHILISM (the belief that nothing is morally wrong).

Criticisms

- Hare does not comment on the content of moral beliefs; someone can assert that "it's alright for people to kill each other" so long as he universalises this and accepts that it's alright for someone to kill him. Hare's morality amounts to little more than consistency: this seems highly dubious.

Response: As a meta ethical theory, it is not necessary to show which morals are right or wrong – that is the job of a NORMATIVE theory.

Criticisms

- People use moral language for things other than commending and commanding, e.g. someone can confess "I shot my mum – it was so wrong of me". If this is a command such as "don't shoot your mum" or a commendation such as "well done for not shooting your mum" then these are only its secondary functions; primarily, it's a confession of wrongness.
- A moral conversation between two people who agree (e.g. that it's wrong to mistreat animals) does not involve them prescribing acts for one another, because they already agree.

Response: Two people who agree are primarily commending an act (the pleasant treatment of animals), and reinforcing their commands to one another not to mistreat animals.

- People frequently do make exceptions for themselves – they think "other people shouldn't do X, but it's OK for me to do it". Hare does not give a convincing reason why we should have to universalise moral principles.
- In the Western world, white people used to think that it was normal and acceptable to enslave black people; we don't think this any more. This seems like MORAL PROGRESS – but prescriptivism cannot view this as moral progress, because moral anti-realists are committed to the idea that there is no mind-independent moral reality. This means that we have not improved our attitudes towards slavery – we've just changed them. We are no closer to understanding moral facts – because there are no moral facts.

Specification content

The following information is from the AQA A Level Philosophy specification, which can be found at:
http://www.aqa.org.uk/subjects/philosophy/as-and-a-level/philosophy-7171

1 Epistemology

1a What is knowledge?

- The distinction between acquaintance knowledge, ability knowledge and propositional knowledge
- The nature of definition (including Linda Zagzebski) and how propositional knowledge may be analysed / defined

The tripartite view

Propositional knowledge is defined as justified true belief:

Issues with the tripartite view including:

- The conditions are not individually necessary
- The conditions are not sufficient - cases of lucky true beliefs (including Edmund Gettier's original two counter-examples)

Responses: alternative post-Gettier analyses/definitions of knowledge including:

- Strengthen the justification condition (i.e. Infallibilism)
- Add a 'no false lemmas' condition
- Replace 'justified' with 'reliably formed' (i.e. Reliabilism)
- Replace 'justified' with an account of epistemic virtue

1b Perception as a source of knowledge

Direct realism

The immediate objects of perception are mind-independent objects and their properties

Issues including:

- The argument from illusion
- The argument from perceptual variation
- The argument from hallucination
- The time-lag argument

and responses to these issues

Indirect realism

The immediate objects of perception are mind-dependent objects (sense-data) that are caused by and represent mind-independent objects

- John Locke's primary/secondary quality distinction

Issues including:

- The argument that it leads to scepticism about the existence of mind-independent objects

Responses including:

- Locke's argument from the involuntary nature of our experience
- The argument from the coherence of various kinds of experience, as developed by Locke and Catharine Trotter Cockburn (attrib)
- Bertrand Russell's response that the external world is the 'best hypothesis'
- The argument from George Berkeley that we cannot know the nature of mind-independent objects because mind-dependent ideas cannot be like mind-independent objects

Berkeley's idealism

The immediate objects of perception (i.e. ordinary objects such as tables, chairs, etc.) are mind-dependent objects

- Arguments for idealism including Berkeley's attack on the primary/secondary quality distinction and his 'Master' argument

Issues including:

- Arguments from illusion and hallucination
- Idealism leads to solipsism
- Problems with the role played by God in Berkeley's Idealism (including how can Berkeley claim that our ideas exist within God's mind given that he believes that God cannot feel pain or have sensations?)

and responses to these issues

1c Reason as a source of knowledge

Innatism

- Plato (i.e. the 'slave boy' argument)
- Leibniz (i.e. his argument based on necessary truths)

Empiricist responses including:

- Locke's arguments against innatism

- The mind as a 'tabula rasa' (the nature of impressions and ideas, simple and complex concepts)

and issues with these responses

The intuition and deduction thesis

- The meaning of 'intuition' and 'deduction' and the distinction between them
- René Descartes' notion of 'clear and distinct ideas'
- His cogito as an example of an a priori intuition
- His arguments for the existence of God and his proof of the external world as examples of a priori deductions

Empiricist responses including:

- Responses to Descartes' cogito
- Responses to Descartes' arguments for the existence of God and his proof of the external world (including how Hume's Fork might be applied to these arguments)

and issues with these responses

The limits of knowledge

- Particular nature of philosophical scepticism and the distinction between philosophical scepticism and normal incredulity
- The role/function of philosophical scepticism within epistemology
- The distinction between local and global scepticism and the (possible) global application of philosophical scepticism
- Descartes' sceptical arguments (the three 'waves of doubt')

Responses to scepticism: the application of the following as responses to the challenge of scepticism:

- Descartes' own response
- Empiricist responses (Locke, Berkeley and Russell)
- Reliabilism

Moral Philosophy

2a Normative ethical theories

- The meaning of good, bad, right, wrong within each of the three approaches specified below
- Similarities and differences across the three approaches specified below

Utilitarianism

The question of what is meant by 'utility' and 'maximising utility', including:

- Jeremy Bentham's quantitative hedonistic utilitarianism (his utility calculus)
- John Stuart Mill's qualitative hedonistic utilitarianism (higher and lower pleasures) and his 'proof' of the greatest happiness principle
- Non-hedonistic utilitarianism (including preference utilitarianism)
- Act utilitarianism and rule utilitarianism

Issues including:

- Whether pleasure is the only good (Nozick's experience machine)
- Fairness and individual liberty/rights (including the risk of the 'tyranny of the majority')
- Problems with calculation (including which beings to include)
- Issues around partiality
- Whether utilitarianism ignores both the moral integrity and the intentions of the individual

Kantian deontological ethics

- Immanuel Kant's account of what is meant by a 'good will'
- The distinction between acting in accordance with duty and acting out of duty
- The distinction between hypothetical imperatives and categorical imperatives
- The first formulation of the categorical imperative (including the distinction between a contradiction in conception and a contradiction in will)
- The second formulation of the categorical imperative

Issues including:

- Clashing/competing duties
- Not all universalisable maxims are distinctly moral; not all non-universalisable maxims are immoral
- The view that consequences of actions determine their moral value
- Kant ignores the value of certain motives, e.g. love, friendship, kindness
- Morality is a system of hypothetical, rather than categorical, imperatives (Philippa Foot)

Aristotelian virtue ethics

- 'The good' for human beings: the meaning of Eudaimonia as the 'final end' and the relationship between Eudaimonia and pleasure
- The function argument and the relationship between virtues and function
- Aristotle's account of virtues and vices: virtues as character traits/dispositions; the role of education/habituation in the development of a moral character; the skill analogy; the importance of feelings; the doctrine of the mean and its application to particular virtues
- Moral responsibility: voluntary, involuntary and non-voluntary actions
- The relationship between virtues, actions and reasons and the role of practical reasoning/ practical wisdom

Issues including:

- Whether Aristotelian virtue ethics can give sufficiently clear guidance about how to act
- Clashing/competing virtues
- The possibility of circularity involved in defining virtuous acts and virtuous persons in terms of each other
- Whether a trait must contribute to Eudaimonia in order to be a virtue; the relationship between the good for the individual and moral good

2b Applied ethics

Students must be able to apply the content of normative ethical theories and meta ethics to the following issues:

- Stealing
- Simulated killing (within computer games, plays, films, etc.)
- Eating animals
- Telling lies

2c Meta ethics

The origins of moral principles: reason, emotion/attitudes, or society

The distinction between cognitivism and non-cognitivism about ethical language

Moral realism

There are mind-independent moral properties/facts

- Moral naturalism (cognitivist) – including naturalist forms of utilitarianism (including Bentham) and of virtue ethics
- Moral non-naturalism (cognitivist) – including intuitionism and Moore's 'open question argument' against all reductive meta ethical theories and the naturalistic fallacy

Issues that may arise for the theories above, including:

- Hume's Fork and A J Ayer's verification principle
- Hume's argument that moral judgements are not beliefs since beliefs alone could not motivate us
- Hume's is-ought gap
- John Mackie's argument from relativity and his arguments from queerness

Moral anti-realism

There are no mind-independent moral properties/facts

- Error theory (cognitivist) – John Mackie
- Emotivism (non-cognitivist) – A. J. Ayer
- Prescriptivism (non-cognitivist) – Richard Hare

Issues that may arise for the theories above, including:

- Whether anti-realism can account for how we use moral language, including moral reasoning, persuading, disagreeing etc.
- The problem of accounting for moral progress
- Whether anti-realism becomes moral nihilism

Possible Exam Questions

Listed below are some possible exam questions. The list is not exhaustive, as other questions can appear on an exam paper. However, it should give you a useful idea of the sorts of questions you might be asked in the exam.

Epistemology

2 mark questions

1. What is reliabilism? *(2 marks)*
2. What is meant by a 'complex idea'? *(2 marks)*
3. What is infallibilism? *(2 marks)*
4. What is *a posteriori* knowledge? *(2 marks)*
5. What is meant by the term 'mind-independent objects'? *(2 marks)*
6. What is empiricism? *(2 marks)*
7. According to Locke, what are the primary qualities of an object? *(2 marks)*
8. What is global scepticism? *(2 marks)*
9. What is indirect realism? *(2 marks)*
10. What is meant by 'sufficient conditions' for knowledge? *(2 marks)*

5 mark questions

1. Explain and illustrate a Gettier-type example. *(5 marks)*
2. Explain the time-lag argument. *(5 marks)*
3. Explain the difference between synthetic truth and analytic truth. *(5 marks)*
4. Explain how indirect realism can lead to scepticism about the existence of mind-independent objects. *(5 marks)*
5. Explain how the tripartite view of knowledge could be enhanced by replacing 'justified' with an account of epistemic virtue. *(5 marks)*
6. Explain why belief might not be a necessary condition of knowledge. *(5 marks)*
7. Explain why the cogito may be an example of an *a priori* intuition. *(5 marks)*
8. Explain how a 'no false lemmas' condition could solve a Gettier-type problem. *(5 marks)*
9. Explain Berkeley's master argument. *(5 marks)*

10. Explain the difference between simple and complex ideas. *(5 marks)*

9 mark questions

1. Outline and explain **two** key criticisms of direct realism. *(9 marks)*
2. Explain the claim that idealism may lead to solipsism. *(9 marks)*
3. Outline Gettier's original **two** counter-examples against the claim that a JTB is sufficient for knowledge. *(9 marks)*
4. Outline and explain the role of philosophical scepticism within epistemology. *(9 marks)*
5. Outline and explain **two** key criticisms of rationalism. *(9 marks)*
6. Outline and explain the tripartite definition of knowledge. *(9 marks)*
7. Explain and illustrate the difference between contingent truths and necessary truths, and how they can be known. *(9 marks)*
8. Explain and illustrate the argument from illusion. *(9 marks)*
9. Outline and explain Leibniz's argument based on necessary truths. *(9 marks)*
10. Outline and explain **one** strength and **one** criticism of indirect realism. *(9 marks)*

15 mark questions

1. Does the external world exist unperceived? *(15 marks)*
2. How convincing is Berkeley's master argument? *(15 marks)*
3. Is there an adequate solution to Gettier-type problems? *(15 marks)*
4. Critically assess the claim that some concepts are innate. *(15 marks)*
5. Can we escape scepticism about the existence of the external world? *(15 marks)*
6. Is knowledge a justified true belief? *(15 marks)*
7. Critically assess whether empiricism demonstrates that all substantive knowledge is derived from experience. *(15 marks)*
8. Is Descartes right to suggest that knowledge must be infallible? *(15 marks)*
9. Critically assess the claim that direct realism accurately explains our perceptions of the external world. *(15 marks)*
10. To what extent are intuition and deduction a source of knowledge? *(15 marks)*

Moral Philosophy

2 mark questions

1. What is error theory? *(2 marks)*
2. What is quantitative hedonistic utilitarianism? *(2 marks)*
3. What is meant by 'moral nihilism'? *(2 marks)*
4. What is eudaimonia? *(2 marks)*
5. What is preference utilitarianism? *(2 marks)*
6. What is Ayer's verification principle? *(2 marks)*
7. What is meant by 'speciesism'? *(2 marks)*
8. What do philosophers mean when they say that 'is' statements cannot entail 'ought' statements'? *(2 marks)*
9. What does Kant mean by a 'maxim'? *(2 marks)*
10. What is the utility calculus? *(2 marks)*

5 mark questions

1. Explain **one** difference between Kantian ethics and virtue ethics. *(5 marks)*
2. Explain why a follower of virtue ethics might view stealing as morally wrong. *(5 marks)*
3. Explain the difference between higher and lower pleasures, according to Mill. *(5 marks)*
4. Explain the difference between cognitivism and non-cognitivism. *(5 marks)*
5. Explain the doctrine of the mean. *(5 marks)*
6. Explain Mackie's argument from epistemological queerness. *(5 marks)*
7. Explain why a preference utilitarian might object to the eating of animals. *(5 marks)*
8. Explain why logical positivists suggest that moral statements are not factually meaningful. *(5 marks)*
9. Explain the second formulation of Kant's categorical imperative. *(5 marks)*
10. Explain why utilitarianism may be seen as a form of moral naturalism. *(5 marks)*

9 mark questions

1. Outline and explain **one** similarity and **one** difference between utilitarianism and virtue ethics. *(9 marks)*
2. Explain and illustrate how the utility calculus can help a moral agent make a decision about stealing. *(9 marks)*
3. Outline and explain Hare's argument that moral statements both commend and command acts. *(9 marks)*
4. Outline and explain how a follower of virtue ethics might approach the issue of simulated killing. *(9 marks)*
5. Explain and illustrate why Nozick's experience machine is a criticism of hedonistic utilitarianism. *(9 marks)*
6. Outline and explain the difference between a voluntary act and an involuntary act, according to Aristotle. *(9 marks)*
7. Explain and illustrate Mackie's argument from queerness. *(9 marks)*
8. Outline and explain what is meant by a 'contradiction in conception' and a 'contradiction in will', according to Kant. *(9 marks)*
9. Outline and explain why refraining from telling lies is a perfect duty, according to Kant. *(9 marks)*
10. Outline and explain the way in which moral naturalism may be said to commit the naturalistic fallacy. *(9 marks)*

15 mark questions

1. Does rule utilitarianism improve upon act utilitarianism? *(15 marks)*
2. Are moral statements just an expression of emotions? *(15 marks)*
3. Critically assess the claim that Kantian ethics provides sufficient moral guidance for agents. *(15 marks)*
4. Is it morally permissible to steal? *(15 marks)*
5. Critically assess the claim that all moral assertions are false. *(15 marks)*
6. Can virtue ethics give adequate moral guidance about the issue of simulated killing? *(15 marks)*
7. Is pleasure the only good? *(15 marks)*
8. When we make moral statements, are we articulating our beliefs? *(15 marks)*
9. Critically evaluate the usefulness of utilitarianism for deciding how to act in **one** of the following issues: telling lies; eating animals. *(15 marks)*
10. Are there any mind-independent moral facts? *(15 marks)*

List of Philosophers

Below is a chronological list of the philosophers whose arguments are contained within this book.

Socrates (469-399 BCE)

Plato (427-347 BCE)

Aristotle (384-322 BCE)

Descartes, René (1596-1650)

Locke, John (1632-1704)

Leibniz, Gottfried Wilhelm (1646-1716)

Cockburn, Catharine Trotter (1674-1749)

Berkeley, George (1685-1753)

Hume, David (1711-1776)

Kant, Immanuel (1724-1804)

Bentham, Jeremy (1748-1832)

Mill, John Stuart (1806-1873)

Sidgwick, Henry (1838-1900)

Prichard, H. A. (1871-1947)

Russell, Bertrand (1872-1970)

Moore, G. E. (1873-1958)

Ross, W. D. (1877-1971)

Stevenson, Charles (1908-1979)

Ayer, A. J. (1910-1989)

Mackie, John (1917-1981)

Hare, R. M. (1919-2002)

Foot, Philippa (1920-2010)

Smart, J. J. C. (1920-2012)

Gettier, Edmund (1927-)

Chomsky, Noam (1928-)

Williams, Bernard (1929-2003)

Diamond, Cora (1937-)

Nozick, Robert (1938-2002)

Goldman, Alvin (1938-)

Parfit, Derek (1942-2017)

Annas, Julia (1946-)

Zagzebski, Linda (1946-)

Set Texts and Further Reading

Epistemology

Berkeley, G. (1713) *Three Dialogues Between Hylas and Philonous*

Cockburn, C. T. (1732) 'A Letter from an anonymous writer to the author of the Minute Philosopher' Appendix to G Berkeley, *Theory of Vision Vindicated and Explained*

Descartes, R. (1641) *Meditations on First Philosophy*, [1-3 and 5-6]

Gettier, E. (1963) 'Is Justified True Belief Knowledge?' *Analysis*, 23(6): pp.121–123

Hume, D. (1748) *An Enquiry Concerning Human Understanding*, [Section 2 and Section 4 (part 1)]

Leibniz, G. W. (1705) *New Essays on Human Understanding*, [Preface and Book 1]

Locke, J. (1690) *An Essay Concerning Human Understanding*, [Book 1 (esp. Chapter 2), Book 2 (esp. Chapters 1, 2, 8 and 14), Book 4 (esp. Chapter 11)]

Plato, *Meno*, [from 81e]

Russell, B. (1912) *The Problems of Philosophy*, [Chapters 1-2]

Zagzebski, L. (1999) 'What is Knowledge?' in John Greco & Ernest Sosa (eds.), *The Blackwell Guide to Epistemology*, pp.92–116

Moral Philosophy

Annas, Julia (2006) 'Virtue Ethics' in David Copp (ed.), *The Oxford Handbook of Ethical Theory*, Oxford: Oxford University Press, pp.515–536)

Aristotle, *Nicomachean Ethics,* [Book 1 (1–5, 7–10, 13), 2 (1–7), Book 3 (1–5), Book 5, Book 6 (1, 2, 5, 8, 9, 12, 13), Book 7 (12–13), Book 10 (1–8)]

Ayer, A. J. (1946) *Language, Truth and Logic* (2nd Edition), New York, Dover, [Chapters 1 and 6]

Ayer, A. J. (1973), *The Central Questions of Philosophy*, London, Penguin, pp.22–29

Bentham, J. (1789) *Introduction to the Principles of Morals and Legislation*, Oxford, Clarendon Press. [Chapter 1 (The Principle of Utility) and Chapter 4 (Measuring Pleasure and Pain)]

Diamond, C. (1978) 'Eating Meat and Eating People' *Philosophy* 53: pp.465–479

Foot, P. (1972) 'Morality as a system of hypothetical imperatives' *Philosophical Review*, 81 (3) pp.305–316

Hare, R. M. (1952) *The Language of Morals*, [Chapters 1, 5, 7, 10.2]

Hume, D. (1739–40) *Treatise of Human Nature*, [Book III, Part 1]

Kant, I. (1785) *Foundations of the Metaphysics of Morals*, [Chapters 1 and 2]

Mackie, J. (1977) *Ethics: Inventing Right and Wrong*, Penguin, [Chapter 1, Sections 8 and 9]

Mill, J. S. (1863) Utilitarianism, [Chapters 1, 2, 4, 5]

Moore, G. E. (1903) *Principia Ethica*, Cambridge University Press, [Sections 6–14]

Smart, J. J. C. and Williams, B. (1973) *Utilitarianism: For and Against*, [Chapter 2 (Act utilitarianism and rule utilitarianism) and Chapter 3 (Hedonistic and non-hedonistic utilitarianism)]

Glossary

A posteriori: something that can only be known through experience, e.g. that grass is green (contrast with A PRIORI)

A priori: something that can be known through REASON (INTUITION or DEDUCTION), e.g. that 2 + 3 = 5 or that 'all bachelors are unmarried' (contrast with A POSTERIORI)

Abductive argument: an ARGUMENT which uses ABDUCTIVE REASONING. if the premises are true, the conclusion is supposedly the best explanation of them (contrast with DEDUCTIVE or INDUCTIVE ARGUMENTS)

Abductive reasoning: an INFERENCE TO THE BEST EXPLANATION – choosing the theory which best explains the data, even though it is not guaranteed (contrast with INDUCTIVE or DEDUCTIVE REASONING)

Ability knowledge: knowing how to do something, e.g. knowing how to ride a bike (contrast with ACQUAINTANCE or PROPOSITIONAL KNOWLEDGE)

Absolutism: theory that morality is inflexible; rules such as "don't lie" apply in every situation throughout time, regardless of circumstances (contrast with RELATIVISM)

Acquaintance knowledge: knowing a person or thing, e.g. "I know Dave" means you recognise him and/or know things about him (contrast with ABILITY or PROPOSITIONAL KNOWLEDGE)

Act-centred moral theories: NORMATIVE theories which focus on what makes an act right or wrong, or what the right act is in a moral dilemma (contrast with AGENT-CENTRED MORAL THEORIES)

Act utilitarianism: CONSEQUENTIALIST NORMATIVE MORAL THEORY which states that the right act is the one which creates the maximum happiness for the maximum number of people; this is decided on a case-by-case basis

Actually impossible: something which is not possible in the real world as we know it, e.g. for a man to jump 100 metres (contrast with ACTUALLY POSSIBLE or LOGICALLY IMPOSSIBLE)

Actually possible: something which is possible in the real world, e.g. for a man to run a marathon in 4 hours (contrast with LOGICALLY POSSIBLE or ACTUALLY IMPOSSIBLE)

Ad hominem: a weak way of arguing which involves criticising the speaker rather than criticising their argument

Affirming the consequent: a logical FALLACY which takes the form: "If P then Q. Q. Therefore P." (contrast with MODUS PONENS)

Agent: a person (also see MORAL AGENT)

Agent-centred moral theories: NORMATIVE theories which focus on what makes an AGENT a morally good person (contrast with ACT-CENTRED MORAL THEORIES)

All possible worlds: every single different variation of how the universe could have turned out. All CONTINGENT truths can be different in another possible world, but NECESSARY truths must remain the same in all possible worlds

Allegory of the cave: Plato's parable to describe the world of the FORMS: slaves in a cave only ever see shadows and they think they're real, until one escapes into reality and realises the shadows were mere copies of real objects

Amoral: one who is neither moral nor immoral – they simply withdraw from morality altogether

Analytically false: a proposition whose falsity can be known *A PRIORI*, simply by understanding the meanings of the words, e.g. "All spinsters are married"; (contrast with ANALYTICALLY TRUE or SYNTHETICALLY FALSE)

Analytically true: a proposition whose truth can be known A PRIORI, simply by understanding the meanings of the words, e.g. "All spinsters are unmarried"; (contrast with ANALYTICALLY FALSE or SYNTHETICALLY TRUE)

Antecedent: the 'if' part of a CONDITIONAL (if-then) statement, e.g. in the statement "If it's Monday, then I have a Philosophy lesson", 'If it's Monday' is the antecedent (contrast with CONSEQUENT)

Anti-realism: see IDEALISM or MORAL ANTI-REALISM

Applied ethics: practical situations which pose ethical dilemmas, e.g. lying, euthanasia, simulated killing, abortion

Arête: another term for a MORAL VIRTUE (see VIRTUE ETHICS)

Argument from analogy: an argument which draws an analogy with some other topic, person or area of study, in order to make a point about the area in question

Argument from disagreement: MORAL ANTI-REALIST view that because people disagree so widely on morality, this suggests that there are no moral facts

Argument from hallucination: criticism of DIRECT REALISM which suggests that a HALLUCINATION is indistinguishable from reality, and therefore we can't know whether our perceptions are real or hallucinatory

Argument from illusion: criticism of DIRECT REALISM which suggests that the appearances of some things are different to the way they actually are, such as a straight rod in water appearing to be bent

Argument from perceptual variation: Russell's criticism of DIRECT REALISM which suggests that a table can appear to be different colours and shapes as the observer moves about the room, yet the table itself doesn't change

Argument from relativity: see ARGUMENT FROM DISAGREEMENT

Argument: provides reasons or evidence in support of a CONCLUSION; a course of reasoning aimed at demonstrating a truth or falsehood; the methodical process of logical reasoning

Assertion: stating something as if it is a fact (sometimes without any evidence)

Attacking a straw man: distorting or misrepresenting your opponent's argument, and then criticising that distorted argument e.g. "Religious people believe in things they can't see, like God, fairies and voodoo, and anyone who believes in fairies and voodoo is mentally ill"

Augment: make bigger and/or better

Begging the question: when the PREMISE(S) in an argument rely on believing the CONCLUSION; when an argument makes an assumption which an opponent would object to, e.g. "I have witnessed a miracle, therefore miracles are real"

Belief: an opinion or view that something is true

Boo-hurrah: refers to EMOTIVISM; the idea that when we say "murder is wrong" or "helping the homeless is morally correct" we're really just saying "murder: boo!" and "helping the homeless: hurrah!"

Brain in a vat: a vat is a jar. The suggestion is that I could be a brain in a jar, being fooled by technology into thinking I'm a walking talking person (see EVIL DEMON)

Cardinal virtues: classical VIRTUES: temperance, courage, wisdom, justice

Categorical imperative: DECISION PROCEDURE for followers of KANTIAN ETHICS; if a MAXIM can 'pass' the categorical imperative, it is morally PERMISSIBLE or praiseworthy. There are three FORMULATIONS: F1 is universal law; F2 is to treat people as ends not means

Causal adequacy principle: Descartes' claim that the cause of something must be at least as real and perfect as the effect

Certainty: a very strongly held belief (see INFALLIBLE beliefs)

Circularity / circular argument: an unsatisfactory type of ARGUMENT where the CONCLUSION merely restates a PREMISE or refers back to the premise, e.g. "An act is wrong if it involves murdering people. Therefore murder is wrong."

Classical utilitarianism: see ACT UTILITARIANISM

Clear and distinct rule: Descartes' rule that 'anything which is clear and distinct is certain'

Closed question: according to Moore, a closed question is one which is only asked if the speaker does not understand the terms involved, e.g. "Are bachelors married?" "Is your dog a mammal?" (contrast with OPEN QUESTIONS)

Cogito ergo sum: Latin for "I think, therefore, I am" – written by Descartes

Cognitivism: META ETHICAL theory that when we make moral statements such as "killing is wrong" we are articulating our beliefs (contrast with NON-COGNITIVISM). Cognitivists are usually MORAL REALISTS

Commensurability: measurability

Common-sense realism: supportive term for DIRECT REALISM (contrast with NAÏVE REALISM)

Competent judges: Mill argued that anyone who has experienced both HIGHER and LOWER PLEASURES would be competent enough to judge that higher pleasures are the best pleasures

Complex ideas: the sensation of something which has multiple qualities – e.g. a fish which is grey, smooth, slippery; we can create new complex ideas by combining IMPRESSIONS we've already had – e.g. a blue giraffe with wings (contrast with SIMPLE IDEAS)

Concept empiricism: the theory that all concepts (e.g. the concept of yellow, beauty, geometry, etc.) are derived from experience

Concepts: ideas such as God, elephants, beauty, space, wrongness; these might be experienced directly via the senses, or pieced together from a range of experiences

Conclusion: the end point of a logical ARGUMENT or SYLLOGISM; usually appears as the last line, and often indicated by the word 'therefore'

Conditional: an if-then statement such as "If you love your wife, then don't hit her"

Conflict of duty / virtues: if we have the DUTY / VIRTUE to tell the truth, but also not to upset people, then what should we do if telling the truth would upset someone? We have a conflict of duty / virtues

Consequent: the 'then' part of a CONDITIONAL (if-then) statement, e.g. in the statement "If it's Monday, then I have a Philosophy lesson", 'then I have a philosophy lesson' is the consequent (compare to ANTECEDENT)

Consequentialism: NORMATIVE THEORY which says the right act is the one which produces the best consequences

Contingently false: Something which is false, but it could have been true, e.g. "York is the capital of the UK"; you can only know it's false A POSTERIORI (contrast with CONTINGENTLY TRUE or NECESSARILY FALSE)

Contingently true: Something which is true, but it could have been false, e.g. "London is the capital of the UK"; you can only know it's true A POSTERIORI (contrast with CONTINGENTLY FALSE or NECESSARILY TRUE)

Contradiction: a statement which makes two incompatible claims, or says something which cannot be true because it is a paradox e.g. "This wheel is not a wheel" or "Everything has a cause, but God is uncaused"

Contradiction in conception: part of Kant's CATEGORICAL IMPERATIVE which states that if a MAXIM cannot be UNIVERSALISED then it is a contradiction in conception (also called a contradiction in the law of nature) (also see PERFECT DUTY)

Contradiction in the law of nature: see CONTRADICTION IN CONCEPTION

Contradiction of the will: part of Kant's CATEGORICAL IMPERATIVE which states that if we will a MAXIM, then we will its end and well as its means – e.g. never helping others, when UNIVERSALISED, means that no one would ever help me. One day I may need help, and therefore I should help others sometimes; helping others is an IMPERFECT DUTY

Cosmological argument: argument that God must exist because everything is caused by something else, and if we work backwards to the first cause of everything, that first cause is God

Counter-example: an example which disproves (or aims to disprove) a theory or ARGUMENT

Decision procedure: the way in which a NORMATIVE THEORY advises MORAL AGENTS to act

Deductive argument: an argument which uses DEDUCTIVE REASONING. If the argument is VALID, then if premises are true, the conclusion is guaranteed to be true (contrast with ABDUCTIVE or INDUCTIVE ARGUMENTS)

Deductive reasoning: working something out using logic, so that the answer is guaranteed e.g. working out that 32 + 47 = 79; we don't need to count out 79 counters to check if it's true (contrast with ABDUCTIVE or INDUCTIVE REASONING)

Denying the antecedent: a logical FALLACY which takes the form: "If P then Q. Not P. Therefore not Q." (contrast with MODUS TOLLENS)

Deontology: a DUTY-based approach towards NORMATIVE ethics which focuses on the intentions of an action; an action is right if the agent is fulfilling his moral duty – the consequences are irrelevant (contrast with CONSEQUENTIALIST / TELEOLOGICAL approaches)

Dependency thesis: what is right or wrong depends on the nature of the society

Direct realism: realist theory of perception which states the world is exactly as we perceive it to be (contrast with INDIRECT REALISM or IDEALISM)

Disjunction: an either-or statement such as "Either the real world exists, or it's all an illusion"

Diversity thesis: because of the diversity of moral beliefs across and within cultures there cannot be one true morality (see ARGUMENT FROM DISAGREEMENT)

Divine command: moral theories which are given to us by God, e.g. the 10 commandments

Divine revelation: God giving knowledge to humans through some sort of religious experience

Doctrine of the mean: Aristotelian theory which forms part of VIRTUE ETHICS; the MORAL VIRTUE is the mid-point between two VICES, e.g. cowardice and foolishness are vices, but in between them is the virtue of courage

Dubitable: able to be doubted (contrast with INDUBITABLE)

Duty: the moral necessity (OBLIGATION) to act a particular way

Egalitarian: treating everyone equally

Emotivism: NON-COGNITIVIST, MORAL ANTI-REALIST META ETHICAL theory that when we say moral statements such as "murder is wrong" we are expressing our emotions about murder, i.e. that we don't like murder (see BOO-HURRAH theory)

Empiricism: theory that all of our knowledge comes from experience; we are born as a TABULA RASA (contrast with INNATISM or RATIONALISM)

End (not means): treating someone as an 'end' involves treating them well because you value them as a human being (contrast with MEANS) (see KANTIAN ETHICS)

Entail: in a DEDUCTIVE ARGUMENT, PREMISES must entail (logically ensure) the conclusion for the argument to be VALID; e.g. the premises 'All crows are birds' and 'All birds are animals' entails the conclusion 'All crows are animals'

Epistemic problem: a criticism of UTILITARIANISM: we can't know whether an act has maximised happiness, because the effects of an act continue indefinitely into the future

Epistemic virtue: see VIRTUE EPISTEMOLOGY

Epistemological queerness: Mackie's notion that if MORAL FACTS were to exist, they would be different from all other facts in the universe, because they cannot be known through intuition or by examining evidence – this makes them 'queer' (see ERROR THEORY)

Epistemology: the branch of philosophy that investigates the origin, nature, methods, and limits of human knowledge

Error theory: COGNITIVIST, MORAL ANTI-REALIST META ETHICAL theory that whether we say "killing is right" or "killing is wrong", they are both false because there are no MORAL FACTS

Eschatological verification: the notion that we can discover the truth of a proposition after death, e.g. it will become clear to us in Heaven that murder is wrong

Esse est percipi: Latin for "to be is to be perceived" (see IDEALISM)

Ethics: the study of morality

Eudaimonia: human flourishing; said to be the ultimate goal of VIRTUE ETHICS

Evil demon: a devil-like being who is powerful enough to trick all of my senses, to fool me into thinking I am a human living on earth – when really I'm not (see BRAIN IN A VAT)

Experience machine: Nozick's idea that if we were offered the chance to plug into a machine and be constantly happy, we wouldn't do it as it wouldn't be real

Explicit premise: premises which are laid out in writing (contrast with IMPLICIT PREMISE)

External world: everything which exists – or appears to exist – beyond my mind

Fact-value distinction: the notion that there is a genuine difference between factual statements such as "Decapitation causes death" and value statements such as "It's wrong to decapitate people", and the former cannot entail the latter (see IS-OUGHT GAP)

Factually meaningful: stating facts

Fake barn: an example where Henry sees a barn and has a JTB that it's real. It *is* real, but there were also lots of fake barns around that area, so it was just luck that he noticed the only real barn (also see GETTIER EXAMPLE)

Fallacy: mistaken or faulty reasoning

Fallacy of composition: assuming that because some things share a feature, that the group of them as a whole has that feature, e.g. "Every person has a mother, therefore there is someone who is the mother of everyone"

Fallible: capable of being false, e.g. a person performing mental arithmetic is fallible (contrast with INFALLIBLE)

Fallibilism: theory that a JTB can be considered knowledge even if it can be rationally doubted (contrast with INFALLIBILISM)

False dilemma: a DISJUNCTION (either-or statement) where the two options being presented are not really the only two options, e.g. "Either you have children, or you despise children"

Falsification: proving something false

Fecundity: whether pleasure will lead to more pleasure (see UTILITY CALCULUS)

Felicific calculus: see UTILITY CALCULUS

First cause: if everything is caused by something which happened before it, then there must be a first cause, which caused everything else, namely, God (also known as the COSMOLOGICAL ARGUMENT)

Forms: Plato's idea that the things we see on Earth are inferior imitations of a perfect 'Form', e.g. we see examples of beautiful things, but beauty itself is UNIVERSAL and only found in the world of the Forms

Formulation: 'section' or 'part'; Kant put forward three formulations of his CATEGORICAL IMPERATIVE

Foundational beliefs: SELF-EVIDENT beliefs; other beliefs or knowledge can be built upon foundational beliefs

Gettier problem: an example in which an agent has a JTB which is not knowledge; this demonstrates that the supposedly SUFFICIENT CONDITIONS for knowledge are not really sufficient

Global scepticism: doubting the existence of everything, including the EXTERNAL WORLD and your own body; this is a method of finding INFALLIBLE beliefs (contrast with LOCAL SCEPTICISM)

God: often taken to mean a being that is all-good, all-seeing, all-powerful and eternal

Golden mean: a VIRTUE which is in between two VICES (see DOCTRINE OF THE MEAN)

Golden rule: the Christian ethic which states "Do unto others as you would have them do unto you" i.e. treat others as you would like to be treated

Good will: according to Kant, the good will involves acting solely out of duty

Greatest happiness principle: the UTILITARIAN PRINCIPLE OF UTILITY, i.e. the right act is the one which creates the greatest happiness for the greatest number of people

Habituation: developing a skill through practice, until it becomes automatic

Hallucination: having sense data (usually visual) of something which is not there

Hedonic calculus: see UTILITY CALCULUS

Hedonism: the pursuit of happiness above all else

Hedonistic utilitarianism: see QUANTITATIVE HEDONISTIC UTILITARIANISM or QUALITATIVE HEDONISTIC UTILITARIANISM

Higher pleasures: according to Mill, pleasures of the mind such as studying philosophy (contrast with LOWER PLEASURES)

Hume's fork: Hume divided knowledge into RELATIONS OF IDEAS (ANALYTIC, NECESSARY, A PRIORI truths) and MATTERS OF FACT (SYNTHETIC, CONTINGENT, A POSTERIORI truths)

Hume's guillotine / law: see IS-OUGHT GAP or FACT-VALUE DISTINCTION

Hypothetical imperative: a CONDITIONAL (if-then) command such as "If you want to be promoted, be nice to your boss" (contrast with CATEGORICAL IMPERATIVE)

Hypothetical reasoning: an argument which rests on a hypothetical (fictional) example

Idea: according to Hume, an idea is a memory of a perception (contrast with IMPRESSION)

Idealism: anti-realist theory that the EXTERNAL WORLD only exists when it is perceived – but it is perceived all the time by God, so it always exists (contrast with DIRECT or INDIRECT REALISM)

If and only if: a way of stating NECESSARY AND SUFFICIENT CONDITIONS, e.g. 'the game is over if and only if the referee says so'. It is stronger than simply saying 'if', because 'the game is over if the referee says so' still allows that there can be other ways for the game to be over

Iff: shortened form of IF AND ONLY IF

Illusion / illusory perception: any perception which is not real, e.g. a hallucination, dream, or trick of the eye

Immaterial: non-physical and not made of matter (contrast with MATERIAL)

Immaterialism: the theory that only minds and their ideas exist, i.e. nothing physical exists (sometimes used to refer to IDEALISM)

Immediate perceptions: whatever the mind experiences directly e.g. SENSE DATA (contrast with MEDIATE PERCEPTIONS)

Impartiality: being unbiased / objective

Imperfect duty: according to Kant, these are duties which don't apply all of the time (we have some choice over how to fulfil them), e.g. we should help others at least some of the time, but we needn't do it all of the time

Implicit premise: an assumption or premise which is not laid out in writing, but exists in the mind of the author and/or reader; also called a suppressed premise or implied premise (contrast with EXPLICIT PREMISE)

Impressions: experiences we are having from our SENSE DATA, or from our own thoughts (see OUTWARD IMPRESSIONS and INWARD IMPRESSIONS)

Incommensurable: unmeasurable

Incompatibilism: theory that belief and knowledge are mutually exclusive – if you know something, you don't (merely) believe it

Incredulity: doubt about a particular fact, against a backdrop of confidence in knowledge generally (contrast with SCEPTICISM)

Indirect realism: realist theory of perception which states that although objects exist in the external world, we can't perceive them directly; we only perceive SENSE DATA directly

Indubitable: something which cannot be doubted; it is 100% certain (contrast with DUBITABLE)

Inductive argument: an ARGUMENT which uses INDUCTIVE REASONING. If the premises are true, the conclusion is likely to be true (contrast with ABDUCTIVE or DEDUCTIVE ARGUMENTS)

Inductive reasoning: working something out based on evidence or experience, but the conclusion is never certain, e.g. no people have ever had blue skin, so it's fairly safe to conclude that the next person I meet will not have blue skin (contrast with ABDUCTIVE or DEDUCTIVE REASONING)

Infallibilism: theory that a proposition is knowledge IFF it is an INFALLIBLE belief (contrast with FALLIBILISM)

Infallible: impossible for it to be false (contrast with FALLIBLE)

Inference: to work logically from PREMISES towards a CONCLUSION

Inference to the best explanation: arguing that a particular theory is the best explanation for the data, compared to other theories (see OCKHAM'S RAZOR and ABDUCTIVE REASONING)

Infinite regress: something which goes on and on for ever

Innate: an idea, concept or knowledge which is within a baby's mind from birth, and doesn't need to be learned through experience

Innatism: theory that we are born with some INNATE knowledge (contrast with EMPIRICISM)

Intellectual virtues: virtues of the mind, such as wisdom and technical skills

Intermediate conclusion: a CONCLUSION that can be drawn from PREMISES, but is not the final end point of the argument (i.e. one or more conclusions will follow)

Intrinsic value: something being good in itself

Intuition: a feeling of being correct about something; more than just a gut feeling, it is the grasping of a SELF-EVIDENT truth

Intuitionism: theory that we can know MORAL FACTS through INTUITION (see NON-NATURALISM)

Invalid argument: an argument where the CONCLUSION is not ENTAILED by the PREMISES, e.g. John is a man, therefore Mary likes sandwiches

Involuntary acts: according to Aristotle, involuntary acts are done unknowingly, where the agent is unaware of some vital information about the situation; we cannot be held morally responsible for such acts (contrast with VOLUNTARY or NON-VOLUNTARY ACTS)

Inward impressions: our feelings and thoughts at the moment they are happening (contrast with OUTWARD IMPRESSIONS)

Irrealism: see IDEALISM or MORAL ANTI-REALISM

Is-ought gap: the notion that 'is' statements such as "Sadie is upset by killing" cannot entail 'ought' statements such as "You ought not to kill Sadie's family" (also known as Hume's guillotine, Hume's law, the naturalistic fallacy, or the FACT-VALUE DISTINCTION)

JTB: JUSTIFIED TRUE BELIEF

Justification: the supporting evidence for a belief

Justified true belief: Plato suggests that this is the definition of knowledge

Kantian ethics: DEONTOLOGICAL NORMATIVE THEORY put forward by Kant, centred around the CATEGORICAL IMPERATIVE

Lemma: a belief or assumption that is used to support a PREMISE (see NO FALSE LEMMAS)

Local scepticism: doubting one particular field of study, such as aesthetics (contrast with GLOBAL SCEPTICISM)

Logic: working something out in a formal, pre-defined way so as to not make any mistakes

Logical form: the structure of an argument, revealed by replacing all the subjects and PREDICATES with variables, e.g. X is a Y, All Y's are Z's, therefore X is a Z

Logical positivism: a logical approach towards philosophy which asserts the VERIFICATION PRINCIPLE as a criterion of meaningfulness

Logically impossible: something which cannot be conceived of or imagined, e.g. a 3-sided square, or that 2 + 3 = 10 (contrast with LOGICALLY POSSIBLE or ACTUALLY IMPOSSIBLE)

Logically possible: something which can be conceived of and imagined, even if it isn't actually possible, e.g. for a man to run a marathon in 4 seconds (contrast with LOGICALLY IMPOSSIBLE or ACTUALLY POSSIBLE)

Lower pleasures: according to Mill, bodily pleasures such as eating, drinking, and sex (contrast with HIGHER PLEASURES)

Material: physical and made of matter (contrast with IMMATERIAL)

Matters of fact: one of the categories of knowledge according to HUME'S FORK; matters of fact are SYNTHETIC, CONTINGENT, A POSTERIORI truths (contrast with RELATIONS OF IDEAS)

Maxim: an intention to act, or a belief about one's moral actions such as "It is acceptable to lie to protect someone's feelings"

Means (not end): treating someone as a 'means to an end' involves using them and not valuing them as a human being, e.g. only being nice to someone so as to get presents from them (contrast with END) (see KANTIAN ETHICS)

Mediate perceptions: whatever the mind experiences indirectly (e.g. perhaps we only experience the EXTERNAL WORLD indirectly, via our SENSE DATA) (contrast with IMMEDIATE PERCEPTIONS)

Meta ethics: the study of what people are doing when they make moral claims, and the study of the nature of moral reality (whether MORAL FACTS exist)

Metaphysical queerness: Mackie's notion that if MORAL FACTS were to exist, they would be different from all other facts in the universe, because they would motivate us – this makes them 'queer' (see ERROR THEORY)

Metaphysics: the branch of philosophy that investigates things that are 'beyond physics', i.e. the nature of reality, what exists, and what it is like

Mind-dependent: things which depend on the mind for their existence, e.g. my memories or things I imagine cannot exist if my mind ceases to exist (contrast with MIND-INDEPENDENT)

Mind-independent: things which do not depend on the mind for their existence, e.g. mountains will still exist even if all beings with minds are wiped out (contrast with MIND-DEPENDENT)

Modus ponens: a VALID ARGUMENT which 'affirms the ANTECEDENT'; it takes the LOGICAL FORM "If P then Q. P. Therefore, Q"

Modus tollens: a VALID ARGUMENT which 'denies the CONSEQUENT'; it takes the LOGICAL FORM "If P then Q. Not Q. Therefore, not P"

Moral agent: any human adult with a normal intellect, i.e. anyone who is able to make moral decisions

Moral anti-realism: META ETHICAL theory that there are no MIND-INDEPENDENT MORAL FACTS; right and wrong are just opinions

Moral exemplar: a person who is really morally good, and sets a shining example of how a MORAL AGENT ought to behave

Moral facts: supposedly MIND-INDEPENDENT facts such as "killing is wrong" or "saving babies is good"

Moral naturalism: see NATURALISM

Moral nihilism: the belief that nothing is morally wrong

Moral non-naturalism: see NON-NATURALISM

Moral progress: the idea that our moral systems are improving, and getting closer to ideal morality; that we are understanding more MORAL FACTS as time goes by

Moral realism: META ETHICAL theory that MORAL FACTS exist: right and wrong are not simply opinions

Moral virtue: according to Aristotle, commendable personality traits such as courage, temperance, kindness (see VIRTUE ETHICS)

Naïve realism: a dismissive term for DIRECT REALISM (contrast with COMMON-SENSE REALISM)

Nativism: the theory that some concepts are INNATE and not derived from experience – however, experience is required to trigger them

Natural facts: normal facts such as 'Peter stabbed Neha', 'Neha is bleeding', and 'Neha is dead' i.e. VERIFIABLE facts about the universe

Naturalism: COGNITIVIST, MORAL REALIST META ETHICAL theory that MORAL FACTS exist, and can be discovered by looking at evidence; moral facts are simply NATURAL FACTS

Naturalistic fallacy: see IS-OUGHT GAP

Necessarily false: something which is false, and it could not have been true, e.g. that triangles have 5 sides; you can know it's false A PRIORI (contrast with NECESSARILY TRUE or CONTINGENTLY FALSE)

Necessarily true: something which is true, and it could not have been false, e.g. that triangles have 3 sides; you can know it's true A PRIORI (contrast with NECESSARILY FALSE or CONTINGENTLY TRUE)

Necessary and sufficient conditions: condition(s) which are needed, and are enough to satisfy something, e.g. having a teaching qualification is both necessary and sufficient to allow you to be a teacher (see IF AND ONLY IF)

Necessary conditions: a condition which is needed in order to do something, e.g. it is necessary to be able to write in order to pass a degree – but it is not SUFFICIENT (i.e. you need more than just the ability to write)

Nihilism: see MORAL NIHILISM

No false lemmas: a condition which can be added to JTB in order to avoid GETTIER PROBLEMS; it requires that the PREMISES (and conclusion) cannot be based on false assumptions

Non-cognitivism: META ETHICAL theory that ethical statements don't have a truth-value (contrast with COGNITIVISM); non-cognitivists are usually MORAL ANTI-REALISTS

Non-naturalism: COGNITIVIST, MORAL REALIST META ETHICAL theory that MORAL FACTS exist, but they are not reducible to NATURAL FACTS; instead, they can be known via intuition (see INTUITIONISM)

Non-voluntary acts: according to Aristotle, non-voluntary acts are done knowingly, but the agent does not truly intend the consequences (e.g. Sharon hits a person because she is forced to do so); we should not be held morally responsible for such acts (contrast with VOLUNTARY or INVOLUNTARY ACTS)

Normative (moral) theory: a moral theory which tells you how to act, e.g. UTILITARIANISM, KANTIAN ETHICS, VIRTUE ETHICS

Normative ethics: the study of moral action

Objective: unbiased and impartial

Obligation: the moral necessity (DUTY) to act a particular way

Obligatory: something which must be done (out of moral DUTY)

Ockham's (or Occam's) razor: the idea that non-essential elements of a theory should be removed; the best explanation is the simplest one which uses the fewest assumptions, and the least reliance on supernatural entities

Ontological argument: an A PRIORI argument which tries to show that the very definition of God is proof that He exists, e.g. God by definition is perfect, and a perfect being must exist because not existing would be an imperfection, so God must exist

Ontological reductionism: when the claims in one domain (e.g. morality) can be reduced without loss of meaning into claims within another domain (e.g. NATURAL FACTS)

Ontology: the study of existence, reality and the nature of being, i.e. trying to find out what exists

Open question: according to Moore, a speaker can meaningfully ask an open question while understanding the terms within the question, e.g. "Is Zach a bachelor?" "Is your dog friendly?" (contrast with CLOSED QUESTIONS)

Open question argument: Moore suggests that "Is X good?" will always be an OPEN QUESTION, no matter what we substitute for 'X' ("Is happiness good?" "Is kindness good?" "Is generosity good?")

Ought implies can: notion that when we say an 'ought' statement like "Bob ought to save the baby", we are implying that he is able to do so. It would not be right to say "Bob ought to save the baby" if Bob is dead, paralysed, far away, etc.

Outward impressions: our SENSE DATA at the moment they are occurring (contrast with INWARD IMPRESSIONS)

P: just as *x* and *y* are often used in mathematical formulae, P and Q are often used in philosophical ARGUMENTS presented in STANDARD FORM (potentially any letters can be used though); P often stands for a PROPOSITION (see S)

Perception: anything we can sense (perceive), usually through the 5 senses

Perceptual variation: see ARGUMENT FROM PERCEPTUAL VARIATION

Perfect duty: according to Kant, perfect duties apply all the time; they are things we must *never* do, e.g. 'don't steal', and 'don't lie' are perfect duties (contrast with IMPERFECT DUTIES)

Permissible: acts which are acceptable; they are neither praiseworthy nor blameworthy, e.g. eating a sandwich, watching TV, walking

Possible worlds: other ways in which reality could have turned out (see ALL POSSIBLE WORLDS)

Practical ethics: see APPLIED ETHICS

Practical wisdom: a VIRTUE which allows a MORAL AGENT to weigh up and decide what to do in a moral dilemma

Predicate: a property of something; part of a PROPOSITION or claim which describes the SUBJECT, e.g. in the sentence "The table is square", 'is square' is the predicate

Preference utilitarianism: CONSEQUENTIALIST NORMATIVE MORAL THEORY which states that the right act is the one which satisfies the preferences for the maximum number of conscious beings

Premise: a claim, reason or PROPOSITION which forms part of an ARGUMENT, e.g. "Tyler is a man" and "All men are human" are premises which ENTAIL the CONCLUSION "Tyler is human"

Prescriptivism: NON-COGNITIVIST, MORAL ANTI-REALIST META ETHICAL theory that when we say moral statements such as "genocide is wrong" we are prescribing (commanding) an action ('do not murder')

Prima facie: a Latin phrase meaning 'on its first appearance' or 'at first glance'

Prima facie duties: according to Ross, DUTIES which we have unless they are outweighed by some other more important factors

Primary qualities: according to Locke, qualities which are the same for every perceiver, such as quantity, shape, size, and mass (contrast with SECONDARY QUALITIES)

Principle of utility: the right act is the one which creates the maximum happiness for the maximum number of people (see UTILITARIANISM)

Process reliabilism: a response to GETTIER PROBLEMS which states that knowledge is a JTB where the justification was obtained through a reliable process

Propinquity: how long we will have to wait to experience happiness (see UTILITY CALCULUS)

Proposition: a statement of fact (or which attempts to be factual) such as "Bachelors are unmarried", "There are four lights", or "Cows make milk"

Propositional knowledge: factual knowledge; knowing that something is the case, e.g. knowing that Paris is the capital of France, or that Debbie is wearing blue socks today (contrast with ACQUAINTANCE KNOWLEDGE or ABILITY KNOWLEDGE)

Pseudo-proposition: something which makes grammatical sense, but is not VERIFIABLE (according to LOGICAL POSITIVISTS) e.g. 'the mind is a prison boiling over with fearsome rainbows'

Push-pin: a simple child's game from Bentham's time

Q: see P

Qualitative hedonistic utilitarianism: Mill's UTILITARIANISM, where it is the quality of happiness (HIGHER PLEASURES) which determines whether the act is right (contrast with QUANTITATIVE HEDONISTIC UTILITARIANISM)

Quantitative hedonistic utilitarianism: Bentham's UTILITARIANISM, where it is the quantity (amount) of happiness which determines whether the act is right (contrast with QUALITATIVE HEDONISTIC UTILITARIANISM)

Queerness: strangeness; Mackie suggested that if moral facts were to exist, they would be EPISTEMOLOGICALLY QUEER and METAPHYSICALLY QUEER)

Question-begging: see BEGGING THE QUESTION

Rationalism: theory that knowledge can be derived from INTUITION and DEDUCTION (contrast with EMPIRICISM)

Realism: see DIRECT REALISM, INDIRECT REALISM, or MORAL REALISM

Reason: logical thinking as a way of acquiring knowledge (as opposed to experience)

Reductionism: making something simpler or easier to understand, or translating it into different (easier) terminology (see ONTOLOGICAL REDUCTIONISM)

Relations of ideas: one of the categories of knowledge according to HUME'S FORK; relations of ideas are ANALYTIC, NECESSARY, A PRIORI truths (contrast with MATTERS OF FACT)

Relativism: theory that morality is flexible and variable: what is right for the UK in the 21st century may not be right elsewhere or in another time period (contrast with ABSOLUTISM)

Relevant alternatives: with a JUSTIFIED TRUE BELIEF, you should consider any other explanations for your belief, e.g. you see what looks like an orange, and you believe it is an orange, but relevant alternatives are that it is made of plastic, it's a hallucination, it's a hologram, etc.

Reliabilism: theory that a PROPOSITION is knowledge IFF it is a JTB where the justification was obtained from a reliable method

Reliabilist virtue epistemology: branch of VIRTUE EPISTEMOLOGY which focuses on how reliable the agent's abilities are, such as their eyesight and intelligence (contrast with RESPONSIBILIST VIRTUE EPISTEMOLOGY)

Representative realism: see INDIRECT REALISM

Repugnant conclusion: a criticism of QUANTITATIVE HEDONISTIC UTILITARIANISM, that the 'best' way to maximise happiness is to have a really overpopulated world even if each person is only a little bit happy, as this outweighs the quantity of pleasure from a happier, smaller population; this sort of world is unattractive

Responsibilist virtue epistemology: branch of VIRTUE EPISTEMOLOGY which focuses on the character traits of the agent, such as how determined and focused they are (contrast with RELIABILIST VIRTUE EPISTEMOLOGY)

Rule utilitarianism: NORMATIVE MORAL THEORY which states that the right act conforms to a rule which, generally speaking, has been shown to create the maximum happiness for the maximum number of people

S: a letter often used to mean 'subject' (person) in arguments presented in STANDARD FORM (see P)

Scepticism: doubting an entire field of study, or more than one field of study; used as a tool to obtain INFALLIBLE beliefs (see GLOBAL SCEPTICISM or LOCAL SCEPTICISM)

Secondary qualities: according to Locke, qualities which vary depending on the perceiver, such as taste, smell, sound, and colour (contrast with PRIMARY QUALITIES)

Secular: non-religious

Self-evident: beliefs or PROPOSITIONS which can be known to be true simply by considering them, e.g. that 3 is larger than 2

Sense data: information gathered from the five senses i.e. sights, sounds, smells, tastes and how things feel (to the skin)

Simple ideas: a single sensation such as redness or squareness (contrast with COMPLEX IDEAS)

Simulated killing: pretend killing, e.g. within video games, TV programmes, plays, movies etc.

Slippery slope argument: a weak way of arguing which involves the claim that if we permit a small (negative) act, it will lead on to greater (negative) acts, e.g. if we allow children to buy lottery tickets, it will lead to them becoming gambling addicts

Solipsism: the theory that I am the only mind in existence

Sophistry: using clever but faulty arguments to deceive or trick opponents

Sound argument: an argument which follows a VALID FORM, and the PREMISES are true (therefore the CONCLUSION must also be true)

Speciesism: treating creatures less favourably simply because of their species (i.e. treating animals less favourably than humans)

Standard form: a way of setting out ARGUMENTS, either by numbering or bullet pointing the PREMISES and CONCLUSION ('C' may be used for the conclusion)

Straw man: see ATTACKING A STRAW MAN

Subject: the item or person that a PROPOSITION is about, e.g. in the sentence "The table is square", 'the table' is the subject

Subjective: biased and based on opinions

Substantive: word used by RATIONALISTS, INNATISTS and EMPIRICISTS to mean meaningful, significant truths about the world; truths which are not ANALYTIC, TAUTOLOGICAL, or mathematical

Sufficient conditions: conditions which are enough for something, e.g. having a degree in Food Safety is enough to qualify you to do the washing up in a café, but it is not NECESSARY (i.e. you don't *need* to have the degree in order to do the washing up)

Supererogatory: something that 'goes above and beyond the call of duty'; something morally praiseworthy, such as saving a child from drowning in a stormy sea

Syllogism: a three line ARGUMENT consisting of two PREMISES and a CONCLUSION, including a major premise ("All X's are Y"), a minor premise ("This is an X"), and a conclusion ("Therefore this is a Y")

Synthetic a priori: a PROPOSITION which can be known through reason alone (A PRIORI) but is SUBSTANTIVE knowledge; it is not merely an ANALYTIC, TAUTOLOGICAL, mathematical or trivial truth

Synthetically false: a proposition which is false, but its falsity cannot be known simply by understanding the meanings of the words – you also need to know something about the world, e.g. "Prince Charles has two daughters" (contrast with SYNTHETICALLY TRUE or ANALYTICALLY FALSE)

Synthetically true: a proposition which is true, but its truth cannot be known simply by understanding the meanings of the words – you also need to know something about the world, e.g. "Prince Charles has two sons" (contrast with SYNTHETICALLY FALSE or ANALYTICALLY TRUE)

Tabula rasa: Latin for "blank slate" – what EMPIRICISTS say our mind is like at birth

Tautology: a PROPOSITION which is just repeating itself, e.g. "A hippo is a hippo"

Teleological: a theory which focuses on the end of something – within ethics, a teleological theory focuses on the consequences of an action (contrast with DEONTOLOGICAL)

Time-lag argument: criticism of DIRECT REALISM which suggests that we don't see things as they are now, as it takes time for the light to reach our eyes, so when we see stars, we're seeing them as they used to be

Trademark argument: Descartes' argument that because he has the idea of a perfect God, this idea must have come from God himself, who put the idea into Descartes' mind to let him know who made him (this is based on the CAUSAL ADEQUACY PRINCIPLE)

Tripartite definition of knowledge: a definition which states that knowledge is a JUSTIFIED TRUE BELIEF

Truth-apt: something that is truth-apt has the possibility of being true e.g. "Today is Tuesday" is truth-apt, whereas "Hello, how are you?" and "Today is a wonderful day!" do not seem truth-apt

Truth-tracking: Nozick's response to GETTIER PROBLEMS; a belief is truth-tracking if S believes that P, and in the closest possible world where not-P, S would not believe that P

Truth-value: whether a PROPOSITION is true or false, e.g. "The author of this book owns a blue car" has a truth-value because it's either true or false, whereas "Marmite is revolting" doesn't have a truth-value – it's just an opinion

Tyranny of the majority: when minority viewpoints are ignored, or the rights of minorities are violated, simply because the majority of people want it that way

Universal law: Kant's first FORMULATION of the CATEGORICAL IMPERATIVE, namely that if we want to do something, we should consider whether there would be a contradiction if everyone acted that way

Universalisability: whether or not something can be universalised i.e. can everyone do the same act?

Universals: timeless, perfect concepts such as beauty and justice, which Plato suggests exist in the world of the FORMS

Utilitarianism: CONSEQUENTIALIST NORMATIVE MORAL THEORY which argues that the right act is the one which creates the maximum happiness for the maximum number of people

Utility calculus: according to Bentham this is a way of measuring (predicting) the happiness that an act will cause; it includes intensity, duration, certainty, PROPINQUITY, FECUNDITY, purity, and extent of pleasure

Utility: happiness (according to Bentham)

Valid argument: an argument where the CONCLUSION is ENTAILED by the premises, i.e. if the premises are true, the conclusion *must* be true too (but if the premises are false, the conclusion might be false) e.g. "All fish are vertebrates, Goldie is a fish, therefore Goldie is a vertebrate" is valid

Valid form: an argument which is VALID when its PROPOSITIONS, SUBJECTS and PREDICATES are replaced by letters, e.g. "All P is Q, Q is R, therefore P is R" is a valid form

Veil of perception: a criticism of INDIRECT REALISM, that we can only experience our SENSE DATA, because we're trapped behind the veil of perception and can't ever get at the world directly

Veridical perceptions: real perceptions i.e. perceptions that are not HALLUCINATIONS or tricks of the eye

Verifiable in principle: knowing what evidence it would take to check the truth of a statement (even if that evidence could never practically be gathered)

Verification principle: rule put forward by VERIFICATIONISTS such as Ayer, that a statement is only factually meaningful if it is ANALYTICALLY TRUE or it is VERIFIABLE IN PRINCIPLE

Verificationism: theory which puts forward the VERIFICATION PRINCIPLE

Vice: a morally bad character trait such as greed, selfishness, cowardice (contrast with VIRTUE)

Vienna Circle: a group of LOGICAL POSITIVISTS working together in Vienna, Austria during the 1920s and 30s

Virtue: a morally good character trait (see INTELLECTUAL VIRTUES and MORAL VIRTUES)

Virtue epistemology: a response to GETTIER PROBLEMS; a proposition is knowledge IFF it is a JTB obtained by someone skilled at finding things out

Virtue ethics: NORMATIVE MORAL THEORY which states that we should work towards developing positive character traits, by following MORAL EXEMPLARS and practising our VIRTUES, to achieve EUDAIMONIA

Voluntary acts: according to Aristotle, voluntary acts are done knowingly and intentionally, and we can be held morally responsible for such acts (contrast with INVOLUNTARY or NON-VOLUNTARY ACTS)

Waves of doubt: Descartes' ideas about ways his perceptions may not be VERIDICAL (his senses can fool him, he may be dreaming, an EVIL DEMON may be tricking him)

Index

A priori / a posteriori: 9, 24-26, 53, **54-55**, 56, 65, 67, 70-71, 112
Abductive arguments: 8, **12**, 13-14, 39, 48, 73
Ability knowledge: 28
Absolutism: **77**, 81, 86, 89
Acquaintance knowledge: 28
Actually possible / impossible: **52**, 53
Ad hominem: 18
Affirming the consequent: 10, **16**
Allegory of the cave: 62
Analytic truths: 9, 26, 35-36, **53-56**, 65, 68, 71, 73, 116-117
Animals: 8, 11, 15, 48, 60, 79, 84-86, 90, **95-98**, 100, 107, 122
Antecedent: **10**, 17, 87
Anti-realism: see *Idealism* or *Moral anti-realism*
Applied ethics: 76, 95-105
Argument from disagreement: **107**, 110, 112, 118
Argument from hallucination: **46**, 50
Argument from illusion: 21-23, **44-45**
Argument from perceptual variation: 45-46
Arguments for the existence of God: 16, **68-70**
Aristotle: 57, **91-94**, 95, 98, 108, 110
Assessment objectives: 19-20
Attacking a straw man: 17-18
Ayer, A. J.: 44-45, 113, **116-119**
Begging the question: 15
Belief: 28, **29-31**, 32-42, 51, 57-74, 106-122
Bentham, Jeremy: **78-81**, 108-109
Berkeley, George: 43, 48, **49-51**
Categorical imperative: **87-88**, 89-90, 98, 100, 102-103, 104-105
Causal adequacy principle: 69
Chomsky, Noam: 62-64
Circular argument: **15**, 40, 93
Clear and distinct rule / ideas: 65-66, 70
Cockburn, Catharine Trotter: 48
Cogito: 26, **65**, 66-67, 70
Cognitivism: 106, **108-115**, 119
Complex ideas: 57-58
Consequent: 10, 16, 87
Consequentialism: 76, 78, 81, 89, 95, 99, 101-102, 104
Contingent truths: **53-56**, 71
Contradictions: **15-16**, 53, 63, 87, 90, 94-95, 98, 100, 103, 105, 121
Cosmological argument: 69-70
Decision procedure: **76-77**, 78, 80, 89, 94
Deductive arguments: 8, 10, **11**, 13-14, 39, 56, **64-68**, 70, 107
Denying the antecedent: 10, **17**
Deontology: **76**, 86-90, 94-95. 102, 104
Descartes, René: 35-36, 50, 60-61, 64-66, 68-74
Direct realism: 21-22, 43-47
Doctrine of the mean: **92-94**, 103, 110
Eating animals: 95-98
Emotivism: 58, 106, 108, **116-119**
Empiricism: 24-26, 49, 56, **57-60**, 63, 64, 67, 68, 73-74
Epistemic problem: 81, 86, 99
Epistemological queerness: 114-115
Epistemology: 27-74
Error theory: 106, **113-115**
Evil demon: 49, 65, 71-74
Exam: 5-7, 19-26
Experience machine: 84-85
External world: 42-51, 57, **70-71**

Fact-value distinction: see *Is-ought gap*
Fake barns: **34**, 35, 37, 39, 40, 42
Fallacies: 10, 14-18
- Ad hominem: 18
- Affirming the consequent: 10, **16**
- Attacking a straw man: 17-18
- Begging the question: 15
- Circular justification: **15**, 40, 93
- Contradictions: **15-16**, 53, 63, 87, 90, 94-95, 98, 100, 103, 105, 121
- Denying the antecedent: 10, **17**
- Fallacy of composition: **17**, 110
- False dilemma: 16
- Slippery slope: **18**, 51, 97, 99, 100

False lemmas: 35, **36-37**
Foot, Philippa: 90
Forms: **61-62**, 64
Foundationalism: 65, 73
Gettier, Edmund (Gettier problems): **32-34**, 35-42
- Responses to Gettier problems: 35-42

God: 9, 16, 43, **49-51**, 56, 58, 59, 61-62, 64, 67, **68-70**, 71-73, 114-115, 119
Goldman, Alvin: 34
Hallucination: **46**, 50
Hare, R. M.: 83-85, 120-122
Higher / lower pleasures: **82**, 83, 96
Hume, David: 56, **57-59**, 61, 65, 69, 71, 107, 113, 117
Hume's fork: 56, 65, 71
Hypothetical imperative: **86-87**, 90
Idealism: 43, **49-51**
Ideas / impressions: 57-58
Immediate objects of perception: 43, 47, 49, 51, 57
Imperfect / perfect duties: **87-88**, 102, 104
Impressions / ideas: 57-58
Incompatibilism: 30
Indirect realism: 43, **47-49**, 50, 51
Inductive arguments: 8, **12**, 13-14, 39, 64
Infallibilism: 31, **35-36**, 64, 73
Inference to the best explanation: see *Abductive arguments*
Innatism: 18, 24-26, 31, 56-57, **60-64**, 67
Intuition: 52, 56, **64-68**, 90, **111-113**, 114-115
Involuntary acts: 93
Is-ought gap: **107**, 110-114, 117, 119
Justification: 9, 15, 29-42, 74
Justified true belief: **29-30**, 31-42, 74
Kant, Immanuel: 68, 78, **86-90**, 91, 93-95, 97-8 100, 102-105, 108, 121
Kantian ethics: **86-90**, 91, 93-95, 97-8, 100, 102-105, 108, 121
Language: 23-24, 55, **62-64**, 106-122
Leibniz, Gottfried Wilhelm: 62, 64, 67
Lemmas: see *No false lemmas*
Locke, John: **47-49**, 50, **57-60**, 62-63
Logical positivism: 116-119
Logically possible / impossible: 50, **52-53**, 115-116
Lying: 33, **101-103**
Mackie, John: 112, **113-115**
Meta ethics: 76, 106-122
Metaphysical queerness: 114-115
Mill, John Stuart: 63, **81-83**, 96, 108-110
Mind-dependent / independent: 43, 47-49, 106, 108, 110-111, 113-114, 116, 119, 120, 122
Missing shade of blue: 58-59
Modus ponens: 10, 16
Modus tollens: 10, 17
Moore, G. E.: 110, **111-113**
Moral absolutism: **77**, 81, 86, 89
Moral anti-realism: 106, 113-122

Moral naturalism: 106, **108-110**, 111-113, 115, 119
Moral nihilism: 119, 121
Moral non-naturalism: 106, **111-113**, 115
Moral philosophy: 58, 75-122
Moral progress: 119, 122
Moral realism: 106, 108-113, 118
Moral relativism: 77-78, 81, 99, 101, 104
Naturalism: 106, **108-110**, 111-113, 115, 119
Naturalistic fallacy: 107, 110-111 (also see *Is-ought gap*)
Necessary and sufficient conditions: 16-17, **29-30**, 31-42
Necessary truths: **53-56**, 67, 68, 71
No false lemmas: 35, **36-37**
Non-cognitivism: 106, 115, **116-122**
Non-naturalism: 106, **111-113**, 115
Non-voluntary acts: 93
Normative ethics: **76-95**, 107, 121
Nozick, Robert: **41-42**, 84
Ockham's razor: 51, 64, 115
Ontological argument: 68-69
Open question argument: 110, **111**, 112
Parfit, Derek: 80
Perception: **42-51**, 57-60
Perfect / imperfect duties: **87-88**, 102, 104
Plato: **29-32**, 33-43, 60, **61-62**, 64
Precision: 20, **21-22**, 25
Premises: **8-9**, 10-18, 36, 38, 39, 46, 51, 64-68, 70-71, 107, 113
Prescriptivism: 106, 108, **120-122**
Prichard, H. A.: 112
Prima facie duties: **90**, 112
Primary and secondary qualities: **47-48**, 50
Propositional knowledge: 28-42
Queerness: 113, **114-115**
Rationalism: 24-26, 56, 57, 60, 61, **64-68**, 73
Realism: see *Moral realism*, *Direct realism*, or *Indirect realism*
Redundancy: 22-23
Relativism: 77-78, 81, 99, 101, 104
Reliabilism: 35, **37-39**, 40, 74
Repugnant conclusion: 80, 83
Ross, W. D.: 90, 112
Russell, Bertrand: **45**, 48
Scepticism: 48, 50, 65, 70, 71-74
Senses: 21-22, 38-39, **43-51**, **56-60**, 61, 71-74, 116
Sidgwick, Henry: 110
Simple ideas: 57-58
Simulated killing: 98-101
Singer, Peter: 79, **83-85**, 96-97
Slippery slope argument: **18**, 51, 97, 99, 100
Socrates: 18, **60-61**, 82
Solipsism: 51
Sound argument: 11
Speciesism: 79, **96-97**
Specification: 5-6, 123-128
Stealing: 103-105
Stevenson, Charles: 118
Sufficiency: 32-42
Synthetic a priori: 26, 65, 67, 71
Synthetic truths: 26, 36, **53-56**, 65, 67, 69, 71, 73, 116-119
Tabula rasa: 57, 60
Tautologies: 54, 68, 110-111, 116
Theories of perception: 42-51
Time-lag argument: 46-47
Trademark argument: 61, 69
Tripartite definition of knowledge: **29-30**, 31-42, 74
Truth: 9, 13, 26, 28-30, **31**, 32-42, **53-56**, 60, 63-68, 71, 73-74, 77, 89, 101-103, 106, 109, 112, 115, 117-119, 121
Truth-tracking: 31, 35, **41-42**
Truth-value / truth-apt: 106, 109, 115-118, 121
Tyranny of the majority: 80
Universals: **61-62**, 64
Utilitarianism: **78-86**, 89, 91, 93-96, 99-102, 104, 108-110
- Act utilitarianism: **78-81**, 83-85, 96, 99-102, 104

- Rule utilitarianism: **81-83**, 84-85, 96, 100, 102, 104
- Preference utilitarianism: **83-85**, 97

Utility calculus: **79-80**, 104
Validity: **10-11**, 13-14, 16-17, 64, 66, 70, 107
Veil of perception: 48-49
Verificationism: 64, 109, 113, **116-119**
Vienna Circle: 116-117
Virtue epistemology: 35, **39-40**
Virtue ethics: 89, **91-95**, 98, 100-101, 103, 105, 109-110
Voluntary acts: 93
Waves of doubt: 71-72
Zagzebski, Linda: 28

30804215R00088

Printed in Great Britain
by Amazon